"Most actors pick up a working knowledge of the film set over years of working on it. Steve Carlson's book has shortened that learning curve considerably."
— Ken Lamkin, ASC
D.P. *Frasier / Wings*

"Steve Carlson's book, *Hitting Your Mark* is the only source I know of for an actor to learn about the set and filming process from an actor's point of view. A very needed addition to the new film actor's library."
— Danny Goldman
Top Hollywood Casting Director

"Steve Carlson's book offers a complete, no-nonsense approach to learning the ins and outs of television and film technique from the actor's point of view. It should be required reading by anyone beginning a career in this field."
— John C. Zak
Supervising Producer,
The Bold and the Beautiful

"An entertaining book about all those things you are never taught yet are expected to know when working on a Hollywood set. A must-read for new film actors or stage actors who wish to make the switch from stage to screen."
— Liz Dalling
President, Special Artists Agency

"Steve Carlson has given us a book that is a must read for anyone new to performing on camera. This is a handy reference book that will be useful for years to come."
— Alan Pultz
Director, *General Hospital*

"I so appreciate, as my students will, the solid coaching and positive approach combined with a realistic appraisal of the actor's life when working and when preparing to work. The sense of humor makes it most appealing and readable and the depth and breadth of experience makes its content extremely valuable."
— Diane Carson, Editorial Vice President,
University Film and Video Association

D1018709

"There is nothing quite as valuable as experience. That being the case, Steve Carlson is passing on a tremendous amount of invaluable experience in this book. Sure, you could learn some of this stuff in a classroom, but there are a lot of things that can only come from experience. This book is a must-have for actors looking to improve their craft. If you're wanting to get into film acting — or even if you've done acting and merely want to learn from the experiences of a seasoned professional — *Hitting Your Mark* is definitely worth the cost. They say that experience is the best teacher; consider this book to be a full course."
— *Microfilmmaker Magazine*

"As a screenwriter, it's important to have a grasp of all aspects of film. Steve Carlson's book takes you into all the things an actor has to deal with, in an interesting and fascinating way."
— Matthew Terry, Screenwriter/Teacher
Seattle Central Community College

HITTING YOUR MARK

2nd Edition

MAKING A LIFE – AND A LIVING –
AS A FILM ACTOR

Steve Carlson

Published by Michael Wiese Productions
11288 Ventura Blvd., Suite 621
Studio City, CA 91604
(818) 379-8799 Fax (818) 986-3408
mw@mwp.com
www.mwp.com

Cover Design: MWP
Book Layout: Gina Mansfield
Editor: Paul Norlen

Printed by McNaughton & Gunn, Inc., Saline, Michigan
Manufactured in the United States of America

© 2006 Steve Carlson

Library of Congress Cataloging-in-Publication Data

Carlson, Steve, 1943-
  Hitting your mark : making a life-- and a living-- as a film actor /
Steve Carlson.-- 2nd ed.
     p. cm.
  ISBN 1-932907-12-2
  1. Motion picture acting. I. Title.
  PN1995.9.A26C37 2006
  791.4302'8--dc22
                              2005030103

To my wife, Mary Ann, without whose support, patience, and ideas this book never would have been written. And to my son, Quinn, of whom I am so proud.

I love you both.

TABLE OF CONTENTS

CONTENTS

INTRODUCTION

The response to the first edition of this book, Hitting Your Mark: What Every Actor Really Needs to Know on a Hollywood Set, was not exactly what I expected. Since I dealt primarily with the technicalities actors face in shooting on film, I expected questions to follow suit.

They didn't. It seems I covered my subject well. The readers and students were interested, appreciative and thanked me profusely... then came the questions.

How do you get started? How do you get an agent? How do you deal with rejection? Can you ever actually feel secure living the life of an actor? Et cetera, et cetera.

I realized I had more work to do.

The first book (and the first part of this one) deals with the unique realities of acting on film. At the time of first writing, there were no classes and few books on the subject. It covers information that is very difficult to come by, yet every actor is expected to know it all the first time they set foot on a set.

Very crucial stuff. But the audience wanted more. Equally as hard to come by is knowing the realities of life as an actor. They wanted to know what to expect, how they could best deal with it and, if possible, prepare for it.

This, I realized, was another area seldom ventured into. Actually, there are very few qualified to even talk about it, only we who have done it.

Let's look at the normal scenario.

The lure of show business usually starts with your first show. Perhaps it was a play in junior high or high school that you got coerced into, or you just wanted to give it a try. Your thoughts at the time, of course, didn't go much beyond that production; hoping you remembered your lines and didn't make too big a fool out of yourself.

But you did it! The accomplishment felt good, the applause sounded great and the gratification was instantaneous. You were going to do this again!

And so you did. Productions in high school, college, or regional theater followed, as perhaps did acting classes and theater arts programs. Perhaps you also got interested in music and/or dance. Everyone's path is different but the mindset is not.

How far can you go? How good can you get? Are you good enough to be a professional? Could you really do this for a living? More classes and productions follow as well as, perhaps, a move of some sort, maybe to where there's a good summer stock program, a repertory theater or even a bigger move to New York or Los Angeles.

As exciting as it all is, what you are trying to do is to get work. Whether it's on film, TV, commercials, a play or whatever, you're auditioning for a job. (You will be amazed to learn how many actors never give much more thought to their careers than just that.)

If you're trying to get cast on film, you might find yourself hampered by a couple of things. The first is that all your training and experience has been on stage. No one ever taught you what to expect on a film set (which is considerably different that a stage). You know nothing about cameras, lighting, or shooting out of sequence. You don't know who all those people around the set are or even what they're doing.

You also don't know where you're going. You want to get this job, then that one, and if you string a few of these together, next thing you know, you've paid the rent for a few months.

If you can keep it up for a few years, you may look back and realize that you've actually made a career for yourself... with hardly any thought at all. In this look back you might also realize that you missed a few opportunities that could have changed your life drastically if you'd only recognized them as opportunities at the time.

How could you have known? There are no rules, no lessons, especially in show business. Many times you never know what's going on from day to day. How can you possibly plan a life or career in an environment like that?

That's what this book is about.

In Book One, we deal with the work itself. What exactly are the differences between acting on stage and on film? It's all "show business" but that's where the similarities stop. The fact that there are both Tonys and Oscars shows that the industry realizes there is a distinct difference between acting on stage and acting on film.

Although each film project is unique, there are certain basics of filmmaking that never change whether you are making a movie, a commercial, a TV series, or a soap opera. You'll learn them here.

This business isn't an elusive mystery but it is a business, and like any other business, people who want to succeed in it should know as much about it as possible.

One of the most important things you'll learn in Book One is what's expected of you as an actor on the set. That's another thing no one teaches but as soon as you step in front of a camera, you are expected to know.

Book Two goes where few books have ever gone before. What is the life of an actor really like? What skills must I have besides being able to act? (You mean, that's not enough?) What is a professional POV and how can I get one? We all know we're going to lose more auditions than we get. Doesn't that get you down? Can I really face this whole thing as a business? How can I set my life up in such a way that will help my career?

We'll also talk about handling money, competition, and enjoying your life off the set. (There's still a person inside there, you know, not just an actor.)

All right, let's get on with it. Sit back, relax and come along as we explore in Book One this most intimate of audiences — "the camera" — and how we, as actors, can please her.

BOOK
ONE

CHAPTER 1

CAMERA, SET, and STAGE BASICS

Before we get fully underway, let's take a moment to go over some basics that every actor should be aware of. Many people are intimidated by a movie set because they don't understand what's really going on. Who are all those people? Before you know how something works it can seem like the most complicated thing in the world. Isn't it amazing how simple things become when you understand them?

Throughout this book we'll be discussing people, places, things, attitudes, and most everything you will need to know about filming and acting for the camera. What follows in this chapter is phase one.

There are certain people every actor should know, or know about, before setting foot on a film set.

DIRECTOR
The director, quite simply, is the boss. Once the shooting schedule begins, everybody works for him.* Since he is responsible for *everything*, all cast and crew alike take their orders from him.

This is the person you talk to if you have any questions about the scene, technical or creative. As an actor, this is also the person you want to make very happy.

FIRST ASSISTANT DIRECTOR
If anyone on the set is busier than the director, it would be the first AD. His job is basically to "run" the set. He makes sure the director's wishes are carried out. He's the one that calls for quiet, activates

---

*When the masculine pronoun is used, it is meant to include both sexes.

1

rehearsals, calls for the camera to roll, notifies cast and crews of breaks, directs extras, and generally keeps the set moving along at a good, healthy, professional pace. It's a tough job.

Still, if you pick your times right, he's usually very accessible for questions.

SECOND ASSISTANT DIRECTOR

Although it's written in singular, there may be many second assistant directors. They take care of much of the logistics on the set. The "second" is the person the actors check in and sign out with each workday. They are also the ones you go to with questions concerning the set, such as getting directions to wardrobe or finding out which dressing room or trailer is yours.

It is also generally the second that you clear it with when you have to leave the set for a few moments. (It's not that they have the authority to release you; it's just that you hardly ever see them without a walkie-talkie, and they will soon either get authorization for you or not. If they find that you are going to be shooting soon, they'll tell you and ask that you don't leave the set.)

It is their job to know where you are.

PRODUCERS

There are many different types of producers, all sorts of levels and echelons that vary from film to film which we won't go into here. Just know that these are the "money guys." These are the people that bring all the various aspects of filmmaking together so the picture can be made.

They put the script with a director, help cast the roles, hire a production company to shoot it, make distribution deals to sell the picture

(TV rights, cable, tape, etc.), and figure out a way to pay for the whole thing.

Actors generally don't run into producers that much but when you do — be nice!

STAGE DIRECTIONS

As we progress through the book, we will run into many things which are not taught since it's assumed that everybody knows about them. Stage directions, however, are certainly taught and since this is the language in which the director will be speaking to you, it's good to have a working knowledge of them. Some of these are unique to film, some aren't. Let's take a quick look at the basics.

UPSTAGE This is the area of the set or stage that is toward the back, or the furthest away from the audience or camera. (The name comes from the practice of having the stage "raked," where the back of the stage is higher than the front, allowing the audience to see much more of the stage area. The back of the stage is literally "up.")

DOWNSTAGE The area of set or stage that is closest to the audience or camera.

STAGE RIGHT & LEFT This is right or left as the actor sees it. (as he looks toward the camera).

CAMERA RIGHT & LEFT This is right or left as the camera or director sees it.

CROSS This is when an actor moves from one point to another in the set.

CROSS DOWNSTAGE When the actor passes between the camera and the object or person specified.

CROSS UPSTAGE When the person or object being passed is between the actor and the camera.

CU Close-up

POV (Point of View) As if the camera were looking through the eyes of a character. We see what the character sees (as seen by...).

PAN The camera moves side to side horizontally, pivoting on its base.

TRACKING SHOT The camera may not pivot at all, but the entire camera itself moves on a "dolly" alongside some action (such as a long walk).

BG Background.

TAKE When they actually "roll film." (The order is blocking, run – through, rehearsal, and "take.")

PRINT When the director likes a take well enough to want to see it (more on this later).

ACTION This is the director's order to start the scene.

CUT This is the director's term for ending the scene. (Note that I am saying "the director's term." Officially starting and stopping the scene is the director's job only. Cameras will continue to roll and actors should remain in character until he says "cut.")

Well, that's enough to get us going. Lots of other terms, phrases, and titles will be dealt with as we come upon them in subsequent chapters.

LINES (DIALOGUE)

It seems strange to me that this subject even has to be dealt with but it is, believe it or not, a problem. One of, if not the primary "given" is that when actors show up for work on the set they *will* know their lines. This is so basic it seems absurd to have to mention it, but you would be surprised how many actors don't. (Also, have you ever noticed how you may see an actor once in something, then never see him again?)

Knowing your lines is the first stage and the most basic step in creating your performance. How can you work on subtleties of delivery if you're hunting for what you're going to be saying next?

This was made clear to me very simply but effectively when I was a young actor working with James Whitmore. I had the good fortune of working with him a few times, and you won't find a nicer man or a more competent, professional actor.

We were working on a movie called *Nobody's Perfect*, a Universal quickie starring Doug McClure, Nancy Kwan, Mr. Whitmore, and me. Mr. Whitmore and I were talking about the business and life in general as we walked through this elaborate Japanese garden that had been built in the sound stage. It was perfect; grass, ponds, knolls, plants, ferns, and lanterns. The set designers had even gone so far as to have "tuning rocks" in the trickling stream.

After admiring the intricacy and complexity of it all, Mr. Whitmore said quietly, "Now tell me, how can an actor show up on the set and not know his lines?"

Short, sweet, and to the point — but I never forgot it. Fortunately, that wasn't a problem of mine!

Remember, besides simply being the professional thing to do (since it is, after all, your job), it also provides an outstanding degree of freedom. Not having to worry about your lines frees you to totally immerse yourself in creating your character and performance.

WHAT DOES HE WANT?

This is an oft-asked question on the set, "he," of course, being the director. This is the person you must please. If you have questions about what he is after in respect to your performance, ask him. Simple as that. A confused actor will give a confused performance. The director will be glad to help you, but listen closely to what he says and don't overdo it. His time is precious. The director is the last word for *everyone* on how a scene and, eventually, the picture will look.

Another way for an actor to get an idea of what types of performances the director is looking for, is to simply listen. Eavesdrop. Hear the directions he gives to other actors. Realizing that the dynamics of each character are unique, don't take other actor's instructions for yourself. However, looking at the picture as a whole, knowing what he wants from another character, may help give you an idea of what he expects from yours.

ATTITUDE

One thing that cannot be ignored on a film set is the crush of people that occupy it. There are a lot of specialized positions necessary in the making of a movie. The fact that there are so many people involved makes it even more important for everyone to work together. If that many people were to lose their central focus, the result could be a mess — an expensive mess!

A healthy, open attitude is one of the primary and most appreciated attributes you can bring to the set. Show business attracts many different types of personalities. You may be dealing with outrageous egos, insecurity, pomposity, brilliance, incompetence, arrogance, "too many cooks"!

Sometimes this leads to difficult situations that are hard to anticipate. Remember that you always want to be part of the solution, never part of the problem. Know your part, do your part, be as "user friendly" as possible, and "above all, do no harm."

YOUR JOB
One common mistake actors new to a film set often make is to try to be too helpful.

Say, the director mentions that he'd like a table close to you moved over a couple of feet. A prop man from the other side of the sound stage starts walking over, but you are much closer to the table than he is.

Should you be a good person and say, "Here, I'll move it," and move the table for him? Absolutely not!

That may seem strange to most of us actors who came from years of school productions and summer stock where we did everything: designed the sets, built and painted them, set the lighting, then tore everything down after the production was over. Generally, we chipped in whenever we could.

Not here! Remember all those people around the set we were talking about? Each has a specific job. Unless personally asked, moving that table is a job for a prop man or a grip. If you do it, you are doing their job and it will be appreciated by no one (especially if a leg happens to fall off the table, or you spill something in the process).

Film sets are insured quite heavily, but you are not insured for any injury that may occur from you moving that table — the prop man is.

Also, if you were to get injured in some freak way by trying to help, it would be much harder replacing you in the film (especially if you'd already filmed quite a bit) than it would to replace a grip. They'd have to go back and reshoot everything you'd already done and no one

7

would be pleased. (Needless to say, this doesn't exactly help the actor's chances of being rehired by this company either.)

Be helpful, be courteous and aware, but be helpful in the carrying out of *your* job and allow the crew to do theirs — they will do the same for you. In professional filmmaking, the atmosphere may not seem as openly supportive and demonstrative as it was in school or "little theater." Actually, it is, it's just different. Just as professional sports don't have the emotional "rah-rah" aspect to them as much as high school or college sports do, it's still there. The difference is, instead of raw emotion, the pros are driven by a professional desire for excellence — to be the best of the best. They are still supportive, but they might not be as openly emotional about it.

Acting for a living, day after day, year after year, the pros' support usually ends up as professional pride in what they do. A feeling that they fully expect you to have also.

Never forget, please, that professional filmmaking is a business. Some sets and some situations are still great fun, but most of the time it's just a bunch of very qualified people setting out to do their jobs well and expecting you to do the same. Everybody wants you to do a good job... for different reasons.

The producers want you to do a good job because it shows they made the right choice in casting you. The director wants you to do a good job because it shows that he's doing a good job directing.

Your fellow actors want you to do a good job because we all learned a long time ago that we do better work when we're working with someone good. Even the camera and support crews are behind you because if *you* look good, they look good.

Sometimes a film crew looks like a collection of different, disparate groups (and sometimes they are), but they all have one thing in common; they all want a good film to come out of this day's work. Plus, if they and everybody else on the set perform successfully, chances are they will all be hired again. (We're back to a *business* again.)

Sometimes there's an even more pragmatic reason for them to be rooting for you — the sooner you get the shot done, the sooner they can go home.

CHAPTER ONE — SUMMARY

Although the producer is the overall boss, the director and the ADs are the ones you will be directly involved with. Remember, your job as an actor is to give the director the performance he wants. Keep an open, flexible attitude and *listen*.

Stage directions are the language of the set. You should know them as well as you know your lines.

Do your job, allow others to do theirs and realize, for their own reasons, everybody wants you to succeed.

CHAPTER 2

TECHNICAL BASICS

As actors, we deal with the camera as a creative entity. Before anybody gets nervous about a motion picture camera, know that there is no difference between it and an ordinary "still" camera, except that the film camera takes a large number of still pictures in rapid succession. When these are projected on a screen appropriately, the impression of continuous motion is produced.

The camera "sees" and records events differently than we see them. The primary difference is that we have two eyes, which gives us "depth perception" or three dimensions. The camera's single eye cannot do that.

Photo courtesy of Panavision

The film, its image, even the screen it's projected on, is flat. Depth, or the illusion of depth, has to be created. This is where the mastery of the filmmakers comes in.

Scenic depth is created by the scene designer, art director, and judicious choices of locations.

Physical depth of a shorter range is created by lighting and choices of lenses.

Physical depth of facial features is created by makeup.

Depth of character is created by the actor and writer.

WHO ARE THOSE GUYS?

Hovering around the camera at any given time is a group you should know about since you'll be working very closely with them. They are *the camera crew*.

DIRECTOR OF PHOTOGRAPHY (AKA Cinematographer)

This individual, usually referred to simply as the DP, is the boss of the camera crew. As such, he is the one most responsible for the "look" and "feel" of the film. Everything from lighting to lenses to which brand of film they should use falls under his responsibility.

Occasionally, he will even help the director with shot selection and camera position.

This is *not* the person an actor goes to with questions.

CAMERA OPERATOR

This is the person that generally comes to mind when you say "cameraman." This is the person who actually looks through the lens and operates the camera. His job is to capture the shot the director has described to him. (Some directors actually will set up the shot in the camera and say something like "Here, this is what I want." It then becomes the operator's job to duplicate that in the actual filming of the scene.)

The operator can be approached by the actor with questions that pertain to the technical aspects of the scene (not concerning performance), such as shot parameters or how fast a certain movement should be made.

GAFFER

The *gaffer* is the head of the lighting crew. His boss is the director of photography. It's the gaffer's responsibility to bring about the wishes and vision of the DP (more later).

FIRST CAMERA ASSISTANT

This crew member is sometimes referred to as the "focus puller." His job is to keep the camera in focus. He will be seen stretching a tape measure from the camera lens to various points where action in the scene will take place. Many times he will ask actors to stand on certain marks to measure the distance so he can be sure of providing a sharp focus. It is then the film actors' responsibility to hit these marks precisely during the scene – more on this in the following chapter).

SECOND CAMERA ASSISTANT

This crew member is the one handling the "clapstick" and the one physically responsible for loading and unloading camera film. Second assistants also bring lenses, filters, and anything else the operator or the first assistant wants.

13

Using the Clapstick

CLAPSTICK

Everybody recognizes the *clapstick* with its diagonal lines and the top *clapper* that claps down to start the scene, but few actually know why. On the slate is the scene number that is being shot and the number of the take that is just about to begin. It is also used by the editor in syncing up sound.

The sound is being recorded by the sound guy over in the corner and the film is being recorded by the camera in the set. The editor has to put those two together. The clapstick shows him where the sound track has to be.

He will take it frame by frame until he brings up the one in which the diagonal lines on the clapper and the body of the slate are in direct line. He will then match that frame with the sound that it made when it was snapped down. The sound will then be synchronized for the scene that follows.

(Most of this is done via computer these days, but you will still see the clapstick, or a variation thereof, on every production.)

In smaller productions there might not be enough money to hire all the people mentioned above, so the jobs combine. Many camera operators also function as DPs. Many times (especially in commercials) a director will also be his own camera operator.

In very small productions, one or two people may do it all.

<<<<<>>>>>

Now, here's a piece of equipment that will follow you around your whole career.

THE DOLLY
In some scenes the camera moves as much as or more than the actors do. Most camera movements are done via the *dolly*, which is really just a camera platform with wheels. This allows the camera, the operator, and the first camera assistant to all move together. In many long "tracking" shots, track is laid down for the dolly like a small railroad to keep the camera moving in a smooth, precise course.

Photo courtesy of Chapman Leonard

Dolly

We will get into the actor's *marks* later but the camera has marks, too — places where it will slow down, stop, and possibly start up again — all in one scene.

15

The control of the dolly and its various moves is in the hands of the *dolly grip*. He pushes and pulls it by hand as fast or as slow as necessary. His job is to get the camera where it has to be swiftly, smoothly, and accurately.

The dolly grip practices his timing, moving the dolly from mark to mark, just as an actor practices his moves, until he is confident that he has them down.

If an actor is involved in a scene that requires a dolly move, he should avail himself of every opportunity to rehearse with the dolly, thereby helping each other to get their moves and timing as soon as possible.

The best thing an actor can do to help when the camera is moving is to make his moves steady and to duplicate them as exactly as possible each run-through. This is not the time or place to try improvising.

There are also other grips on the set, mostly working for props and lighting. As their name implies, these are the hands-on people. They are the ones that do the actual physical moving of props, equipment, and lights.

Their boss is called the *key grip*.

STAND-INS / SECOND TEAM
Other terms that the new film actor might not be familiar with are *first team* and *second team*.

In most professional productions the lead actors have people assigned as *stand-ins*. These are people who match the lead actors in height and coloring. It is not necessary that their genders match.

Though the function of a stand-in is not a difficult one, it is a necessary one. Because of all the lights needed for filming, sets can sometimes get quite hot. It wouldn't be good for the actors to be hanging around the set all the time, getting hot, sweating off their makeup and getting tired, but the lighting people have to have a body in the set to see how to light the scene. Enter the stand-in.

The drill usually goes like this: the actors (first team) are shown by the director what their actions will be in the scene. This time is called "blocking." Watching all this will be the camera operator, the DP, and the stand-ins (second team). After the actors are shown their various moves, the first camera assistant puts down marks (more on them in the next chapter).

When blocking is over, the actors leave to rehearse, go to makeup, wardrobe, rest... whatever. When they leave, the second team steps in on the marks wearing, if not identical clothing, at least a wardrobe with the same general coloring. Since they resemble the leads in height and coloring, light will react the same on them as it will on the actors.

By the time the actors are called back into the set, the lighting is complete, cameras have had a couple of run-throughs with the stand-ins, and everyone is ready for actual rehearsal — theoretically!

A good habit for an actor returning to a set where a stand-in has been substituting, is to ask the stand-in if there have been any changes. The director will show you eventually but since they usually have five or six plates in the air at any one time, directors usually appreciate the fact that you found out on your own and have already been rehearsing the new moves for a few minutes before they are able to come over and give them to you.

One thing to keep in mind — stand-ins are not slaves, servants, or waiters. They don't work for you, they work for the producer and director, the same as you. What they are, generally, are extras who happen to have the same coloring as one or more of the lead actors.

In some cases, especially on TV series, a star's stand-in may also be the "stunt double." This can provide a nice, long-term assignment for the stunt person (or at least as long as the series lasts).

SECOND UNIT

Another term, not to be confused with second team is *second unit*. This is strictly a FYI since second units hardly ever involve actors.

This is a camera unit which is sent to a location without the director. (If he were there, it would be the *first unit*.) Second unit usually consists only of a camera operator, first assistant, and sometimes a gaffer. Their responsibility is to get background exteriors or "cutaways" that can be edited in with the film shot in the studio.

An example:
A young boy looks longingly out his bedroom window.

CUT TO:
A shot of Pikes Peak through a window.

CUT TO:
Boy sighs, then goes to bed.

When it's all seamlessly cut together, there will be no doubt that the boy is looking out his window at the mountain, even though his bedroom is on a set in Los Angeles and Pikes Peak is in Colorado.

The second unit shot that POV shot of Pikes Peak.

COVERAGE

This is the term that refers to the various shots and angles the director shoots so that the editor will have sufficient footage necessary to create a flowing, believable scene (more on this later).

PRINT IT!
Second only to "Wrap" which means the shoot is over, actors love to hear the term "Print it." It shows they must have done something right. Like any camera, a film camera shoots film *negatives*. This means that the film has to be developed before it can be seen. Developing movie film is expensive, so there's no reason to pay to develop shots that didn't work.

The only shots actually developed are those the director instructs the script supervisor to print. That means he likes it enough to look at it, but he still may continue shooting and print four or five others. This is the director's prerogative and each has his own style. (Usually at least two are printed "for protection.")

Our job as actors is to keep doing the scene until the director is happy, which is why we all love to hear the words "Print it!"

Incidentally, since videotape goes directly to a positive image, nothing has to be developed to be seen. It's all available all the time, which makes it much easier and cheaper to work with. Videotape, however, doesn't have the rich depth that film has, which is why all motion pictures and most TV shows are still shot on film. (The notable exception, for speed of editing, are Soap Operas.)

SEQUENCE
Everyone knows that most films are shot out of sequence. In case you don't know exactly why, we'll take care of that right here.

It would certainly be much easier for the actor if we could just start at the beginning of the script and move our way through it, like a play. Actually, the director and AD who set up the shooting schedule try to do that as much as possible, but there are just too many variables for it to happen too often.

First of all, remember again that this is a business in which time (crew, actors, equipment, locations, etc.) is very expensive. If the movie you are doing happens to end in the same location it began, you can count on the beginning and ending of your picture being shot, if not on the same day, at least within a day or two while the crew is still set up in that location.

They're not going to shoot the beginning, leave, have a myriad of other setups, then come back to the same place to end it. It would just be too expensive.

Or if, say, your leading man has a beard in the last shot but not at the beginning. They're not going to wait around for him to grow a beard so they can finish the film! No. In this case, they'll have him growing his beard like crazy before they start shooting (and before they have to pay anybody). They will then shoot the end first along with everything else he has to do with a beard, then cut it off and go back and shoot the beginning.

Another problem film crews have to deal with everyday is the sun. General daylight has to be dealt with constantly. It may take all day to film and fully cover a scene, yet the lighting has to appear the same as it did in the morning when they're still shooting at 5:00 in the afternoon. Lighting guys are pretty good at faking that.

What's very tough for them is when the shot is at dawn or sundown. You might find yourself getting up a few mornings early until the scene gets done just right while the sun is also just right. (Scenes shot in the rain also bring their own unique problems, as you can imagine.)

Multiply the above possibilities a few hundred times, taking into consideration various locations, sometimes even different seasons, hair and weight changes and, of course, the length of various actors' contracts.

Not everyone in a film is hired for the entire shooting period. Actually, very few are, usually only the main leads. Supporting characters can range from one day to several weeks, depending on the size of their role and how long it will take to shoot it.

If an actor has a one-week contract, they'll schedule all his scenes in that one week even if his character reoccurs through the whole picture. And that's just *one* character!

There's no getting around it, film actors just have to learn to shoot scenes out of context.

CHECKING THE GATE

Actually "Print it" is not really the final phrase. When the scene has been satisfactorily done and the director is pleased with his prints, he asks camera to "Check the gate."

Everyone gets very quiet and apprehensive while the first camera assistant takes off the lens and checks the area where it connects to the camera. This is affectionately called "the gate." Occasionally a hair, a piece of lint, dust, sand, or any number of small, barely discernible particles get caught in there. If that's the case, they have to clean the gate and continue shooting because the film they just finished shooting will be no good otherwise.

If any large piece of debris gets caught in the gate, the camera operator will see it and clean it immediately. The particles in question here are too small for him to see but large enough for us all to see once the film is blown up to feature or even television size.

"The gate is clear" are the words that cause everyone to start breathing again.

21

CHAPTER TWO — SUMMARY

Here, we met the cast of characters in the film crew, as well as some of the apparatus you will be working with. Knowing the routine followed in filming, as well as who all those people are and what they're doing, helps make sense of the whole process.

As the scenes are covered, there may be many takes — but they only print the good ones.

For a myriad of reasons, shooting out of sequence is just one of the evils of filmmaking that we have to learn to deal with. The more you understand the technical side of film acting, the more you will appreciate the mosaic it is.

CHAPTER 3

MARKS

WHY?

Focus, in any camera, is predicated on the distance between the subject and the camera and is perhaps the single most important element in filming. It doesn't matter what the shot is, if it's not in focus it's useless.

During blocking, you will become quite aware of this person coming at you from the camera with a tape measure. As previously mentioned, this is the first camera assistant, or the focus puller.

The camera operator's primary responsibility is to frame the shot as perfectly as he can. He is also looking to make sure the lighting is correct and that it stays that way; he and has a myriad of other things to deal with. He doesn't have time to effectively do his job, concentrate on the scene as it progresses, and try to keep the shot in focus at the same time.

The first camera assistant's main job is to keep the shot in focus, but since he isn't looking through the lens, he has to rely on marks and measurements. That's why the first assistant will measure you (and/or your stand-in) at every *mark* in the scene.

The actor is "marked" virtually every time and place he stops in the scene. That place is then measured. In some scenes you may only have one mark, but in a busy scene, you could have many.

Become comfortable with your marks as soon as possible, hit them as precisely as you can, and the camera crew will be your biggest fan. Let's find out how.

The first point of the mark is simply to show where you were standing when they measured your distance to the lens. After that, the mark is to show you where you are to be because that's where you will be in focus.

Marks can range from being chalk marks on the floor to a T made out of gaffer's tape. Some get fancy and have premade cardboard T's (in which you straddle the stem of the T like this:).

If you are stationary and don't have to walk into the shot, they may even give you footprints to stand in.

These are also used when the shot is very close and it's critical that you don't move.

BLOCKING

As we've already learned, blocking is where the actor is given the moves he'll make during the scene. The camera crew watches this closely. They won't disturb you when the director is first giving you your positions, but the first time you walk through it, the first camera assistant will be right there marking you as you go.

If you have a stand-in, the crew will probably spend more time measuring and marking with him, but a lot of productions can't afford such luxuries so you'll find yourself being lit very often.

Don't get your ego in a twist if they ask you to go through your moves many times — it's all a part of the film actor's job.

Remember that not only does the actor move (or, in a large scene, many actors), but the camera also moves, so the relative distance between camera and subject (or subjects) is always changing. That makes hitting your marks very important.

#1-#2-#3

In many scenes, especially longer, more complicated scenes, you may have many marks. These will be numbered 1-2-3, etc., starting from the first, when you first enter the scene, to the last, where you end up.

Remember, though, to always keep flexible. Everything is subject to change. Maybe the shot didn't look as good through the camera as the director thought it would, or the light keeps changing, the moves look awkward, or whatever. Marks are never made in stone.

They may change blocking and reset three or four times before you actually start "putting some down" (rolling film). In those cases you'll be asked, "Could you go to #2 for me?" (etc.) by someone in the camera crew. They will make the necessary corrections, give you your new mark, remeasure you, and try another rehearsal to see if this works better.

This aspect of setting up the shot can sometimes be the most time consuming, but it is also one of the most critical. However marvelous the actor is doesn't mean a thing if he's out of focus.

The camera may have many different marks in a scene also, places where it's supposed to slow down, maybe stop, then start up again to move to yet another mark. During all this the actors are moving about and the first camera assistant is trying to keep the scene in focus. See why so many people in this business have gray hairs?

WHAT CAN I DO?

What you can do to help things along as an actor is to be aware. Pay attention. See where your marks are, know where they are, get comfortable with them, and practice moving from mark to mark in a steady pace. Whether it's fast or slow doesn't matter as long as you do in rehearsal what you do during filming (and vice versa). Be sure to show them what you're going to do at actual performance level. Don't just walk through it. These camera guys are good, but they won't know exactly what you're going to do unless you show them. Work it out for yourself, show them, then stick to it. (If you realize you miscalculated something and want to change it, go to the director and show or tell him what you want to do. If he agrees, he'll have you show the changes to the camera, marks will be changed, and filming will continue.)

HOW TO USE

Okay, so we now know how important hitting your marks is to the camera and how critical it is for focus, but you might be wondering how to use them. They are there on the floor but hardly any scenes have you walking into a scene looking at the floor. So, there they are, but you can't look at them.

To make matters worse, another thing to be aware of is that if the floor shows in the shot, once rehearsal is over and you start shooting for real, the marks come up. (You can't really have a taped T in the middle of your living room carpet, can you?)

If the shot does not include the floor, however, the marks can usually stay. You still can't look at them, but your peripheral vision may be better than you think. Practice it. Looking straight ahead, walk to the edge of a rug and stop right at the end of it.

You might have to practice it a few times, but I think you'll be surprised how close you can come to that edge just relying on your peripheral vision. But you never rely on just one thing alone.

THE "WEB"
The trick is to pay attention to where you are. I mean *really* pay attention. Use your surroundings. Get the *feeling* of your relationship to walls, props (like a chair), windows, even other actors. Build a web of eyelines around you and put yourself in the middle. Practice going from mark #1 to #2, etc., many times. Count how many steps it takes. (Do this at performance level. If you're running in the scene, count them running.)

If it takes three steps to get to your next mark and it's about a foot away from the corner of the sofa, line yourself up with the lamp on the end table and you'll probably be able to hit that spot within two to four inches, and that's close enough for most master shots. (You'll have to be a bit more accurate in CUs.)

If the above rather obvious solutions don't work, you'll have to get creative. Remember, the important thing is to get you to a certain spot where you will be lit and in focus.

One creative approach that comes to mind is to figure out a way to look directly at the mark! You don't want to be staring at the camera or staring at the other actor (usually), but people normally look around, sometimes they look down at their shoes (embarrassed?), or off to the side (where you have a piece of tape on the side of a sofa). Sometimes you have to get sneaky.

The very best way, always, is if you can work it into your character. Why does the character stop in that particular spot? Is he looking out the window? Then take your position from the window. Is he meeting someone? If the other actor is stationary, you can even take your mark from him.

Go back to *feeling* where you are. Become very aware of your relationship to furniture or anything else that's stationary — even the camera.

Another wonderful one that most actors neglect is *light*. You can *feel* when you are well lit. Since that's one of the primary reasons for marks in the first place, you would know that when you feel well lit, you are in focus. (Check this with camera, of course, but 90% of the time, that's where you should be.)

If you feel too far away from stationary objects to get a good mark, try navigation. Line up objects in your line of sight, such as aligning a chair on the set with a lighting pole behind it. Rehearse it a few times. Even using your peripheral vision, you can see when they are aligned. Couple that with your general feeling of space, counting your strides, and anything else you can add to the mix. You'll have a good web, and you'll be on your mark.

OPTIONS

The camera assistants will usually set the marks for you because they know what's going to be in the shot and what's not, but what they come up with may not work for you. If not, then you have to invent something yourself.

Don't be afraid to put a small piece of tape on the inside of a handrail so you'll know exactly where to stop. Or maybe a small dot on a sliding glass window to show you your mark before opening it.

Outside, use the wonders of nature. A twig lying off to one side where you stop on the grass is the perfect mark, and many times it can even stay in the shot. If it's too big, try a couple blades of grass laid sideways to the others. You'll be amazed how easily your peripheral vision will pick that up.

In "big action," chases and such, the actor is generally moving too fast to be kept in a tight frame, so the shot is usually fairly wide. What that means to the actor is that the marks are not that critical. You have to stop in the vicinity of something, not on a dime.

You could stop by the fender of that car or by a light pole or dive behind that rock when they're shooting at you.

Where marks get critical in big action is when they come in for CUs. That's when you put that piece of tape out of sight on the other side of the big rock as you look back to see if they're going to shoot at you again. Or you put a rock by the car fender to show you *exactly* where to put your foot to bring you to where you have to be. (You've practiced this by now, you see.)

EXTREME CLOSE-UP (ECU)
The tighter the shot, the more exacting the marks have to be. In big action you probably have a variance of about a foot; in a regular master shot, about three to four inches. In an ECU, sometimes you have to hit a spot within an inch or less.

Because an ECU is so close, all they usually need to see in the shot is an indication of movement, so many times you will set your position to the camera, lean out a few inches, and gently rock back to your exact spot. It's much easier to hit a crucial spot that way and the shot still sees you stopping from an action. It works.

Stepping into an ECU can be tough. It's too precise for peripheral vision. Here too, you don't want to rely on any one mark in any tight or difficult situation. In a case where the camera is very close, use the camera itself as one arm of your web.

If you're *very* close, sometimes you can use your own reflection in the lens. Find out where they want you exactly, see where you are in the lens and duplicate it. (Of course, this only works in situations in which you are looking *into* the lens.)

Another great help in this ECU situation is using sandbags. These are always around the set because they use them to weight down light stands, shiny boards, filters, etc. Get yourself situated exactly where you have to be for the shot, then place sandbags in front of, and touching, the fronts of your shoes.

If you have to step into a critical scene, have them preset.

Literally, bump up against them. You will know you are exactly where you have to be. (Practice this a number of times. When used in conjunction with general area awareness and some of the other tips we've mentioned, you should be right on the money!)

Focus is at the very core of taking any picture, be it a still or a feature. Any time you are performing any function in a film, marks are going to come into play because focus is always mandatory.

When driving a car, for example, exactly how far away from the center line you are becomes critical because there is a camera car three feet away from you, speeding at seventy miles an hour like you are trying to take your picture! Consider it a mark.

Driving into a driveway, stopping, getting out and walking to the front door requires three to four marks, depending on the camera person.

    1. The car has to stop in an exact spot — variance of maybe two to four inches in any direction.

    2. Where you stand in relation to the car as you get out and retrieve your groceries from the back seat.

    3. Your walk to the front door. If it is a long one, chances are they'll want a mark in the middle (i.e., "keep to this side of the sidewalk, brush against this shrub on your way," etc.).

    4. Where you stop at the front door, hunt for your keys, before opening the door and going inside.

Not particularly difficult stuff, but things to be aware of.

DRIVING

Having a car hit that particular spot may require a bit of practice. I've done quite a bit of precision driving over the years and have come away with the realization that anybody can do it if (1) you are comfortable driving; (2) are a good driver (i.e., smooth and steady); and (3) if you don't mind putting in some practice.

Even if there is a mark down on the driveway, by the time you drive up to it, you can't see it. Also, you have to know how deep your tire is in the wheel well if you're going to hit that chalk mark. Mainly it's just awareness and practice.

Put your tire exactly on the mark they want, then look around. Where do you fit in your surroundings? Build yourself another web of landmarks. You might be five feet from the garage door which is down. OK, that's an approximate. That's not going to help you that much.

31

The camera is directly to your right when you stop, but you're not going to be able to look at it (except peripherally). So it too will help, but it won't get you within the couple of inches you need.

If nothing seems to line up for you, *make* something line up. Have someone take a white stake (chair, light stand, whatever — something you can easily see) and line it up, off camera, for you. Put it in line with, say, your side mirror or the side of the windshield. This is something you can see coming, prepare for as you drive up the drive, and see it getting closer.

If the garage door is out of the shot, you might want to put a piece of tape on it that you can easily see to show you which line to take when driving up the drive. If it's in the shot, find something else.

You might find yourself in a driving situation where you will be following a camera truck. This is probably the easiest markwise because they're in constant contact with you. Lying beside you is a walkie-talkie that is open to the director's channel. He'll tell you if you have to be a little right, a little left, a little closer, etc. You find the relationship to the truck, line up a few things so you know you can continue to hit it, and proceed to dazzle them with your steadiness and professionalism.

HORSES
Being originally from Cheyenne, Wyoming, it was natural that I would end up in some westerns. Fortunately, I came to Hollywood when quite a few were in production and I ended up shooting westerns for about three years.

Trying to hit a mark with a horse I thought would be impossible. In a way it is, so what they do is give you a really big mark.

First of all, movie horses are wonderful. If you are galloping into an area, have to stop and dismount on a mark, the most important thing to do with a movie horse is practice. After you show the horse what you want him to do four or five times, he will usually repeat it for you without you having to worry about it all that much.

Another saving grace is that the camera knows you're not going to be able to stop precisely, so the frame is usually large enough to accommodate a certain amount of dancing around that most horses do. Very seldom would the camera operator be "locked off" (meaning he wouldn't be able to move the camera), so he will be prepared to *pan* with you as you move about.

What we were talking about above is for the master; CUs are another thing. If you have a quiet horse, CUs can sometimes be shot while still on horseback. If you have one that's a bit more frisky, you might have to get a little creative. You may find yourself shooting your CUs while riding the top of a fence (the fence will be below frame, of course).

COMMERCIALS
In shooting commercials we still have to deal with everything we've been going over, but now we add "The Product." In a commercial, the product is the star, so the composition of the shots is going to be reframed to feature the product.

Marks involving the product are *critical*. It doesn't matter so much if you are in soft focus, but the product *cannot* be. It must and will be sharp. If you handle the product, set it down or use it in some manner, your moves will be carefully measured and spots carefully marked.

In this case you build your web around the product, making sure that you can move it or set it down *exactly* where they want.

CUs & ECUs on the product are known as "beauty shots," and they are the most critical of the critical. The director and camera operator will help you practice your product moves and set or suggest marks for you. With what you've learned above, you will be able to supply a few of your own now, too.

One of the most challenging things to do is to hold an object perfectly steady while the camera tries to get an ECU of it. People just naturally shake or move ever so slightly. In an ECU, that "ever so slightly" can look like an earthquake. What you need to do is brace yourself.

Say you are holding a wonderful cup of Folgers coffee. They've shot the master of you at a party, talking with friends, drinking your coffee. Now they're coming in for a CU.

They have filled the frame with the cup, saucer, and your hand holding them — but it's all over the place. The first step in solving this is to see if you can use your surroundings. If you happen to be standing next to a wall, lean on it and push your elbow up solid against the wall. You'll be surprised how solid that makes you. Even if you weren't against the wall in the master, they may be close enough in this shot that the BG doesn't show, so you could scoot over to the wall to shoot it there anyway. (The director will suggest that, by the way — not you.)

Look for a table, chairs, trees, anything in your scene that could help brace you. If all that fails, what they may do is put a C stand under your arm. This is a stand that holds lights and/or filters. They put an arm of this stand under your elbow, which you rest upon it. It also will steady you and since the shot is so tight, the camera won't see it.

Another sometimes difficult camera move is to raise a small object up into a CU (i.e., I've been the spokesman for different credit cards over the years and have had to do this a hundred times). Still, if the shot is superclose, with virtually no margin for error, sometimes we just have to do it a lot of times until one falls into place.

The other day we approached an ECU in a much easier way. We started the shot with me holding the product on camera. We made sure focus was perfect, rolled camera, I held the product a second or two, and then slowly took my hand and the product out of frame. (We did that a few times "for protection.")

What they will then do with that is run the film backwards. It will appear as though I brought it up *into* the frame — and in *perfect* focus!

CHAPTER THREE — SUMMARY

Since even the finest performance means nothing if the actor is not correctly lit and in focus, we learned the importance of marks as well as some tips on how to use them. In all types of shooting, the actor has to get to the right place at the right time. Marks show the way.

Remember the web and keep creative. Most anything can be used as a mark.

CHAPTER 4

GENERAL CAMERA AWARENESS — ONE CAMERA

"One-camera" filming is the kind most people think about when they picture filmmaking in Hollywood. All feature films are shot this way and most TV shows except situation comedies (sitcoms) and soap operas. (These are shot with three cameras which we'll get into in the next chapter.)

Earlier we defined "coverage" as the various angles the director shoots so the editor will have sufficient footage to put together a flowing, believable scene. With one camera, that requires a lot of "setups."

The first shot in one-camera filming is called the *master*. This is a shot that is far enough away to encompass all the actors and action. The entire scene will play in this shot which will now serve as a reference for the coverage (which, technically, is any shot other than the master).

The master is perhaps the most important scene for the film actor because this is where your performance is really created. In subsequent shots, you're basically going to be matching what you establish in this shot — your moves, your actions, your intensity — everything! Now is the time to do it. In blocking the master is also where you will work closest with the director. This is the time to ask any questions you may have or make any suggestions concerning the scene.

After the master is shot, it's too late to change anything drastically because at that point, you'll basically be copying, in any number of angles, what you did in the master.

The general movement of shooting is from the outside in. From the wide master, we move into "three shots" or "two shots," which simply means that if there are a number of people in the scene, we now start focusing in on the ones we want the audience to pay particular attention to.

From the two shot we move in to *over the shoulder* (OTS) shots, which is basically a close-up (CU) but with a portion of another actor's shoulder and back of head. This shot sometimes serves as a CU although it is not quite as close. What it does, though, is to continue to show the relationship between the two actors involved. That proximity can be very important in the telling of certain stories.

Continuing our move closer, we get to the *close-up* itself. This is exactly what it says. Your face now fills the screen. This is not the time to be "caught acting" because every little flicker shows.

We can even move closer with an *extreme close-up* (ECU). This is an extremely tight shot used when something small but specific needs to be shown; i.e., the hint of a telling tattoo that can barely be seen by the shirt cuff of the bad guy. An ECU would be taken of that cuff and portion of tattoo.

MATCHING

From the technical point of view (POV) there is nothing more important for the actor to do than *matching*. As you saw above, the coverage shots are all just closer angles concentrating on smaller parts of the master. The editor has to cut all these snippets together and have it flow.

In order for him to do that, the film actor has to match his motions exactly. If you are playing cards in the master and yell "Gin," throw your cards on the table and light a cigar, in the subsequent coverage you have to do it exactly the same.

If you threw your cards on the table before you yelled "Gin," it wouldn't cut. The editor wouldn't be able to use that shot. Neither could he if the cards you threw out in the CU are different than the ones you threw out in the master; nor if you picked up the cigar with a different hand or lit it differently or if one cigar was smoked down further in the master than the one you picked up in the coverage.

Get creative and think out your scene and performance for the master. Make mental notes of what you're doing and when, knowing you will have to duplicate everything you're doing. (That's actually a good case for keeping things simple. The busier your action is, the more you have to match.)

Incidentally, if the scene is very complicated in terms of matching, and some scenes can certainly get that way, the script supervisors are the ones who can help you. We'll discuss their functions later but for now, know that your matching is part of their responsibility. If you start to pick up the cigar with the wrong hand, they will stop you, refresh your memory as to what you did in the master, and let you try it again.

If you know in advance that you're going to have trouble matching something (such as having a lot of different physical business going on at the same time — smoking, eating, drinking, etc.), mention it to "script" and ask if they can help you. They will appreciate your awareness and be very glad to help.

Script supervisors take copious notes, but they can't be aware of everything. The more you can remember about what you are doing in the master, the easier you make their job, and the more you'll be appreciated as a professional.

EXAMPLE:
Let's look at an example here to see how it all works.

A man and a woman are having dinner at a small table. The first shot, the master, is back far enough to be able to see both actors and the table. They will play out the full scene in this shot.

After that's been done to the director's satisfaction (and he has ordered at least one to be "printed"), he will proceed to "cover" the scene. The next shot will probably be a close-up (CU) of one of them; we'll pick the woman.

This could either be an over the shoulder shot, in which part of the man's head and shoulder shows, or a straight CU of her in which you don't see him at all. The full scene is again played out with this camera configuration with the actors being very careful to match the eating and drinking moves that they did in the master.

When the director feels he has what he wants from that angle, he will do the same coverage on the man in a simple dialogue scene that may be all the coverage necessary. A more involved scene will require more involved coverage: i.e., there is a lounge singer in the BG who's having an affair with our lady. The director will want at least one shot of him. If our man chokes on his wine, we may want an extreme close-up (ECU) of that, as well as her reaction to this.

Even though the ECU would just be for the wine spill, the actors may be asked to do all or part of the entire scene again for this shot, or at least two or three lines before the incident, to give it a running start. Actors always do better if they're fully involved in the scene. For that reason, the actors may find themselves doing the scene many times in order for the director to get the necessary, quality coverage he wants to convey the intent and "feel" of the scene.

It's amazing how one shot can change the feeling and intent of a scene completely. No matter what you were envisioning in the scene above, imagine what a totally different scene would emerge with the same actors, the same dialogue, the same coverage, except this time we add an additional shot — one of a bomb under the table.

As an actor your performance doesn't change a bit. You have to be totally ignorant of this addition (if your character is supposed to be). The camera, coverage, and editing will supply all the suspense needed.

COMMERCIALS

Commercials are also shot using one camera and can be some of the most exacting shooting you'll run into. Consider:

A feature film runs around an hour and a half and usually takes around three months to film (sometimes *considerably* longer).

A TV movie, around two hours long, takes around a month to shoot.

A TV series episode, about an hour, takes around seven days to shoot.

A sitcom, one-half hour long, rehearses for a week, then shoots "live" for one day.

A soap opera, one-half hour or an hour, shoots one show every day.

A commercial, thirty or sixty seconds long, usually takes between one and three full days to shoot (sometimes *considerably* longer).

Also, as strange as it may seem, sometimes the budgets on a sixty-second commercial can approach that of a small feature. (Have I mentioned that this is a *business*?)

41

Advertisers have only thirty or sixty seconds of very expensive air time to convince you how much better your life will be if you buy, use, or invest in their product. They have the time and the money, so they make sure everything is perfect: focus, lighting, subtle innuendoes of meaning, lavish camera pans, everything!

Needless to say, in commercials, another series of shots will be added — product shots. Let's have our dining couple, this time, be doing a commercial for Folgers, having dinner and coffee. The coverage would still be basically the same except the camera angles would be sure to include and feature the coffee cups.

The coverage we had above would then be followed by CUs and ECUs of steaming coffee, a man and woman greatly enjoying their sips, and anything else the director can think of that will convey how absolutely wonderful life can be if only you would drink Folgers Coffee.

We'll get a bit further into the editing process later so you can really see how these various pieces are put together. You know enough now, though, to have an overview in your mind and this will help you. Imagine how the current take fits into the way the scene will end up and how that in turn fits into the picture.

As we deal with individual specifics along the way, let's not forget the primary purpose, and that is, to tell our particular story; to move our audience to tears or laughter but always to *feel*.

As long as the audience is aware that they are watching a movie, we've lost them. We want them inside the movie with us, and they wouldn't be watching the movie if they didn't want that to happen too. It's called the "suspension of disbelief." By coming into the theater, or turning on the TV, the audience is saying, "Okay, I'm willing to buy your premise. I'll go along with whatever you say as long as it makes sense. But if you don't do a good job of convincing me, I'm outa here!"

Audiences today are pretty savvy. They've seen so many films they're not as easily pleased or as easily fooled as people were years ago. Today, it's got to be right. It's got to be smooth. Things have to match. Any hiccup which doesn't track will remind the audience that they are, in fact, watching a movie (and that something didn't work). Once again, we've lost them.

LINE OF AXIS
This is basically a technical FYI. As an actor you won't have to worry about this too much because the director, DP, and script supervisor will worry about it for you. It's referred to as the "180 degree rule" and sometimes can get pretty complicated. What it deals with is how certain moves or actions will cut with other moves and actions.

When the editor puts together all the various shots in each scene, not only do your small, personal movements as an actor within the scene have to match, the big movements of the scene have to match also. Failure to effectively implement this rule can result in people seemingly looking at walls instead of at each other; or a person starting to walk into a room, then suddenly jumping to the other side of the room as he enters. It can be very distracting and totally lose continuity (and your audience) if it's not done right.

Extremely simply put, the camera shoots the master scene from a certain direction. A line, the *axis line*, is then established. All coverage must be shot from the same side of the axis line as the master, if the people are going to appear as though they are actually looking at each other. Crossing that line changes screen direction and makes people appear to be staring out into space.

If a man in his CU is looking at his girlfriend "camera left," when she looks at him in her CU, she will be looking "camera right." If you visualize this, you can see that that would keep both of their coverage shots on the same side of the axis line. These CUs should cut smoothly into the master if everything else has also been matched.

43

Everytime an actor walks in or out of a shot, somebody is very aware of this rule because it's got to fit with the scene that follows, which, as we know, may not be filmed for weeks. As mentioned, copious notes are taken during the run of the shoot.

The director will tell you which side of the camera to leave by or on which side your look should be focused. If there is ever a discussion about this, at least you'll know a bit about what they're discussing. They're trying not to "cross the line."

PARAMETER

In one-camera shooting, the actor should always know what the parameters are of the shot he is about to shoot; by that I mean the size of the frame in the camera. If you walk into a scene, find out exactly where they are cutting you. Where are you in frame and where are you out? It's also helpful to know if they're cutting the bottom of the frame at your knees, your waist, or your chest.

The main reason to know this is to keep yourself in frame. If they're cutting rather tight, you know not to make your movements too large. The larger the frame, the more freedom of movement you have.

It's also important to know the parameters of the shot exactly, to assure that your entrances and exits are clean.

Incidentally, to get this information, just ask. The camera operator is the person you go to with this. A simple question to him — "Excuse me, where are you cutting?" — will do it. He will tell you your parameters. Rehearse them.

Even in a tight frame you should still match your actions from the master. If you were standing with your hands in your pockets in the master, keep your hands in your pockets for your CU, even if they are shooting shoulder-high. The way your shoulders and arms align will not be the same if you just let your arms hang. Film picks up little things like that. Try to be aware of as many of them as you can.

Where knowing your parameters becomes critically important is in dealing with props (or product, as in a commercial). You have to know just how much room for movement you have. When the prop is in the picture. When it is out. How far you move it for it to be cleanly out.

Another situation occurs when you are holding something rather low, like a gun. If they are shooting you at your waist, as you shift weight from one leg to the other, your gun may be popping in and out of frame. This is very distracting to your audience.

Find out where they are cutting and make a choice either to raise the gun up a bit so it's in this shot, or lower it a bit so you don't see it at all. In this case, if a gun is drawn, there is probably a reason for it, so it should probably be shown.

Say, instead, you were holding a pack of cigarettes waist-high and you realize you have to move it one way or another. If the cigarettes weren't actively involved in the scene, you might want to slide them down a couple inches out of the shot and lose them to the camera completely for this angle.

While the choice is yours (and the director's), just realize the importance of knowing the size of the shot because your performance has to either expand or condense to that size. (We'll have more on this later.)

FLAWS
Does the camera really add ten pounds? Sorry to say, but yes it does. What it does actually is intensifies any feature. If you have a large nose, the camera will make it look even larger. If you are too skinny, however, the camera may pick up on the shallow cheekbones, and visible ribs and make you look ill, instead of adding ten pounds and making you look more healthy.

Flaws of many sorts are intensified. Facial blemishes and scars can appear more prominent. A "soft" chin can actually add more than ten pounds. Fortunately, the wonders of makeup can considerably help most of this.

If you are generally fit and healthy, though, you should photograph just fine. Nobody has a perfect face. We all need a little of the cosmetician's brush to get us fully into film shape.

One flaw makeup can't help is posture. A slump you might not even be aware of could make you look like a hunchback or a degenerate. If that happens to be your character, great, keep the slouch, but if that isn't your character, watch your posture. The camera may convey a message about you and your character that you don't want sent.

Know what you are doing, why, and add "posture" to the list of things to be aware of. It's a very easy thing to change, but that doesn't make it any less important. It can seriously alter the way your character is perceived. The camera might make a lot more out of it than you would like.

One-camera shooting is where you have to constantly be aware of matching (in contrast to three camera where the master and coverage are shot at the same time, lessening the need to worry about it.) In order to be able to match effectively in the various covering shots, you have to be aware of yourself and your actions.

CHAPTER FOUR — SUMMARY

In shooting with one camera, the direction of coverage is from the out-side-in (or from the master to the CU). Since these shots have to be seamlessly cut together, matching our movements is one of our key jobs.

Knowing the parameters of each shot is also crucial, for this determines the range and extent of your movement. It also helps to keep in mind how your various coverage shots will be integrated into the whole.

CHAPTER 5

GENERAL CAMERA AWARENESS — THREE CAMERA

As well as continuing to deal with film, we are now also including the realm of videotape. The change to tape doesn't affect the actor all that much except that a little more light has to be pumped into the set. Makeup has to be slightly different to make sure you don't look washed out by all the light, but that will be taken care of for you.

In shooting with "three camera," the big change for the actor is the *types* of things that are shot and the *way* they're shot. In this chapter we'll look into how three camera shooting is used in sitcoms and soap operas. (Game shows, talk shows, and other "hosted" shows which are also shot this way will be handled in the next chapter.)

SOAPS

What shooting with three cameras (or more) allows you to do is to shoot your master and coverage at the same time. In the case of soap operas, which are shot on videotape, the director actually edits the show in the camera while it is being shot.

The director's camera preparation in three camera is to work out the blocking for the various scenes, work out camera locations (which camera should have the master, which a CU, which a two shot, etc.) as well as decide how he wants to edit it.

As you (the actor) walk in the door to join a party, the director may follow you in the master to establish the party. As you approach the hostess, he may cut to the camera holding a closer two shot on the hostess and you. As your ex-girlfriend looks on, he will cut to another camera holding a CU on her.

While this scene is progressing, the cameras reposition to their next shot. The director calls out over their headsets to alert them as to which camera is "hot" (which camera is currently supplying the picture that is being taped).

Each camera operator has a "shot card" which tells him the various shots that he will be responsible for and the order in which they will occur. There are marks for their cameras, too, places where they have to be to assure a good line of sight for their next shot.

The power supply for the cameras comes from large, long cables which also conduct the picture they're taking. Overseeing these cables is a "cable puller," whose job it is to try to minimize the snakelike traffic jam that could result if these cables were left untended.

Who crosses who, when, and where the cables are going to go is also part of the director's job in choreographing the camera's movements.

There are no dollies in soap operas. Each videotape camera is mounted on its own wheeled platform. The camera operator himself rolls the camera to it's various marks. He also focuses the picture himself.

All this is happening as the scene is being shot. A fully edited scene is already "in the can" as the scene ends. If something goes wrong, everybody shoots it again.

I was a member of the original cast of *The Young & the Restless* twenty something years ago. It's amazing to see how tape technology and capabilities have expanded over the years.

In and before the sixties, soaps were broadcast on the air "live"! If you forgot your lines or a wall in the set fell down, you had to start ad-libbing like crazy (just as you would do in a play) until you got the problem solved and got back to the story.

By the time we started "Y & R," technology had progressed to the point that we were taped live. What that meant was that if the set fell down we could cut, put it back up and start shooting again, but we had to go back to the beginning. (By the way, you just *didn't* forget your lines.)

But they still couldn't edit. The only time they could cut tape was during the time they would have to cut away for commercials. If there were two scenes in two different sets that were to be played between commercial breaks, those two scenes would be taped back to back, without a break. Here's one example of how a soap-sound stage can be set up. This example is based on the working stage of *The Bold and the Beautiful.*

SOAP-SOUND STAGE

As the first scene would be completing, one camera would cut loose from the others and roll over to the next set, which would have been built adjacent to the first one. As soon as the first scene ended, the director would cut to the lone camera in the second set as that scene started. The one camera would cover the scene as well as it could while the other two cameras quickly and quietly rolled into position in the second set while the scene continued.

As soon as they were situated, the director would start using their pictures along with the first camera, just as they had rehearsed a number of times earlier. (The camera operators got real good at this stuff.)

Even though an actor may have done a wonderful scene in your first part of the above scenario, if someone happened to make a mistake in the second scene, since they could only cut from commercial to commercial, the cast would all have to go back and redo the entire thing—*both* scenes! As I mentioned, if you forgot your lines too many times (like maybe three times a year), you would be looking for work.

The editor still had to put the scenes together, have music added, and credits and spaces for promos and commercials inserted before sending the tape off to New York for broadcast. A complete show had to be done every day and it was a race every day.

By the time I joined *General Hospital* in the eighties, technology had advanced to such a state that scenes could be reshot if the director felt that a better performance could be achieved. (In the early days, if you remembered your lines and hit your mark, they printed it. They didn't have time for the luxury of going after the best performance.)

Now, it's amazing what they can do. If somebody flubs a line in the middle of the scene, they can go back, reshoot the line, edit it in, and continue on. The whole process takes about two minutes.

The computer age has digitized everything and streamlined videotape production so much that they can even include special effects and location shooting in the same time that they used to have to rush to get a show shot live.

SITCOMS

Even though sitcoms (situation comedies like *Friends*, *Wings*, *Cheers*, *Frasier*, etc.) are also shot with the three-camera method, that's where the similarity ends.

The two major differences are that a sitcom is shot before a live audience, and only one show is shot per week. The actors generally rehearse four to five days and then shoot their show two times on the fifth day (or night). They also have a different audience for each show.

When the second audience is sent home, cast and crew get back to work picking up any odd shots that may have been missed during the actual tapings. These sessions can go into the wee hours of the morning.

SITCOM STAGE LAYOUT

Needing to supply only one show a week, sitcoms don't have the crunch of time that a soap does. They also usually have more money. Some sitcoms are shot on tape but most are shot on film. This means that the three cameras being used are on dollies, shot by a camera operator, and focused by an ever present first camera assistant.

All the film from all the cameras is developed, transferred to videotape where it is edited (they can use the magic of computers with tape), then the film negatives are cut to correspond with the cut tape.

Photo courtesy of Frasier

Preparing to shoot with four cameras

In a soap, the cameras go from set to set. In a sitcom, because everything has to be situated in front of the audience, the sets change instead of the cameras. All this makes doing a sitcom much more like doing a play, but with some significant differences.

The audience is there but it's still a *TV show*. The audience you are playing to is in the camera. You don't project to the live audience at all. Your concern as an actor is the scene as seen by the camera. The audience is there primarily for timing and knowing where the laughs are. It also adds a pinch of adrenaline which brings out better performances in the actors.

The logistics in a sitcom, which can get quite involved, still are easier than a soap since everything is right in front of them. Next time you watch a sitcom, notice how it is written to be played out in one or two sets, like a play. (There will generally be five, six, or more setups in a soap.)

Loading cameras

Photo courtesy of Frasier

Another difference in the two is that most soaps are an hour long (a new show is shot and edited every day), and all sitcoms are one-half hour (with one show filmed each week). Needless to say, the life and work of an actor in these two mediums are quite different.

SIMILARITIES

Although there are major differences in these two art forms, your job as an actor, once you get in front of the cameras, is not all that different.

MARKS

Hitting marks, in both mediums, is more like hitting marks in theater. Rather than being little snippets of scenes, as in film, when your primary concern is focus, here, your concern is creating an entire smooth-running scene.

In many cases, hitting marks is actually more critical here. Since what the cameras are doing, essentially, is taping a play, they don't stop and reposition to get CUs or two shots that have to be gotten as the scene is played out. As such, if you want to be seen, you'd better be on your mark and clear of your other actors when it's time or you've just missed it. They'll simply go to another shot of someone else.

The director will set it up for you in blocking and "run-through." Pay attention not only to your own blocking but also to other actors in your scene. Make sure in rehearsal that they are not blocking you and that you are not blocking them. Remember, if you can see the camera, the camera can see you.

Think of blocking in these mediums as choreography. It really is a dance with you, the other actors in the scene, and the cameras. The audience is not part of this dance, even in the case of sitcoms. They are watching you tape your show. Period. The only acknowledgment you give that they are even there is to wait for their laughs to subside before continuing on.

Actually, there is one other consideration you do make to the audience — you "turn out" slightly to favor the audience like you would in a play, which also favors the cameras since they're right in front of the audience. Notice in sitcoms, like *Friends*, how their furniture is set so the action is played straight-out to the audience.

Even soap sets don't face out that much, though you do have to turn out a bit for the cameras since they are all on one side of the set. (It

56

makes the 180 degree rule no problem at all in either of these types of shooting.) In one-camera filmmaking you may want to turn out a very small bit while filming the master, but it's usually not that big a deal since the camera will be coming around to cover you, no matter how you're facing.

REHEARSAL

In a one-camera film set, all action in back of the camera is stopped for filming. In both soaps and sitcoms, by their very nature, that is not the case. Cameras are constantly in motion, setting up new shots, actors are moving, cable pullers are pulling cable, "boom mikes" are hovering overhead, moving and turning as each actor speaks (more on them later), and in the case of the sitcom you have your audience which may or may not be laughing when you expect them to.

The point is, a lot's going on, and your job is to forget about it and concentrate on what you are doing — acting and telling your story.

In time, as you learn what to expect and that you can deal with the unexpected, this won't be that difficult for you to do. When it's your first few times in this particular arena, however, it can be quite disconcerting.

My suggestion is this — hang out. Spend as much time on or around the set as you can. Watch, see what people are doing, understand why they're doing it. Take the mystery out of it. During rehearsal look around, see where and when the cameras are moving, get as used to that movement as you can. You don't want movement out of the corner of your eye to distract you when you're in the middle of a scene. The more you know what's going to happen, the less distracting it will be.

Besides, your peripheral vision is going to be needed for other things as you shoot. You'll still need it to help you land on your marks accurately; an awareness of the camera will make sure you're clear, and you'll be able to feel if you are in your light as you are supposed to be. (Actually, in some sitcom sets, there might not even be marks. Your position is placed "by the back, left side of the chair," or the "right side of the window," etc.)

Duplicating your movements is as important here as in filming, but for different reasons. Make the same moves at the same pace during taping as you did during rehearsal. The cameras will do the same thing. When you're finally shooting this for real, there should be no surprises.

Incidentally, even though I've mentioned a number of things here, this is not particularly difficult. Read it, think about it, see the logic of it, and let it go. You're not going to have to go through a laundry list of individual things you should be aware of. You'll just find that you know more and are absorbing more. It will all come back to you in your mind under the general heading of "awareness."

SHADOWS

The bane of lighting directors in both of these mediums is shadows. In film we shoot one scene or one portion of a scene from one camera. That shot is lit specifically, then we move on to the next shot and light that one specifically.

In soaps and sitcoms, we're doing a little play. The whole thing, all the moves have to be lit from the beginning. What makes this job even harder is the fact that cameras are constantly moving around to get the best angle for their next shot. In order to permit them the freedom they need, all lights need to be hung from "light bars" above. All lights are "flown."

This has a tendency to throw bizarre shadows if you're not careful. An actor half lit by overhead light is not a pretty sight.

Besides being doubly sure that you hit your mark which will keep you in your light, the next thing to watch out for is shadows on your coactors. Anyone can tell when someone is blocking their light. An experienced actor will simply shift his weight to his other foot or do something which will cause him to drift an inch or so to get clear. (Once you're aware of it, you'll be amazed how easy it is to feel this and correct it without missing a beat.)

One thing that even the best of us can't feel, however, is when our light is blocked, say, up to our mouth. With overhead light, when two people are standing side by side on the same plane, there is always going to be a shadow over at least a portion of one, if not both of their faces.

Actually, it's not a big problem to correct. Once you become aware of the situation, all you need to do is to move up or down stage a few inches until you can see that you're clear. The director will tell you which he would prefer you do. The problem is when your coactor is not aware of the situation.

My suggestion for you here is The Golden Rule. If you mention to your co-actor, "Here, I'll move upstage a bit to get my shadow off your face," do you really think he'll thank you for that and then let *his* shadow cover *your* face? I don't think so.

TELEPROMPTER/CUE CARDS

Teleprompters and cue cards have their own chapters coming up, but I just want to mention something here. "Cards" or "prompters" are very seldom used in sitcoms — remember, they've had a whole week to rehearse a half-hour show — but many soaps still use them.

If you shot twenty pages of dialogue today and have to shoot another thirty tomorrow, your brain might turn to oatmeal somewhere along the line and be glad they are there.

Make sure you notice where the 'prompters are in rehearsal. If they're using cards, the people holding them should also be practicing getting in good positions where they can be seen easiest by the actors. You can always ask them to move a little this way or that so you can see them better. They are there to help you. Don't be afraid to help them help you even more. It's okay.

"THREE-CAMERA" ACTING

In one-camera film there is seldom a doubt whether you are on camera or not. In three camera you never really know so you have to treat the scene like you're doing a play. You've got to be "on" all the time.

Don't think just because someone else is talking that the camera is going to be on them. That's the first thing you would assume, true, but sometimes the *reaction* to something is much more interesting than the saying of it. Keep yourself in character for the whole scene.

Another reason is consideration of your fellow professionals. If you are in the middle of your dialogue and the person you're talking to (in the scene) is looking off in the distance or not paying attention, that would make your job even harder, wouldn't it? You bet it would. It would also be very unprofessional.

It's much easier to stay in character through the whole scene in a sitcom because of the audience. Whether we openly acknowledge them or not, they are still there and we know it. Plus, all the cameras are shooting all the time, and you can never tell for sure which piece they're going to want to use.

So, if you're working as a professional actor, I think you'll find it wise to do the professional thing and keep in character straight through from "action" to "cut."

Speaking of "cutting," these are two out of very few situations where you do not ask the camera operators the size of the shot or where they are cutting you. The reason is, of course, that it's always changing. One camera may be holding a master and another has a CU on you. Thirty seconds later, in the same scene, it might be exactly opposite. I guess you're just stuck having to act with your whole body for the whole scene.

There is a way in soaps to tell if the camera that is pointing at you is hot, but I wouldn't count on it. On top of each camera is a red light. When the director is taking his "feed" from that camera, the red light goes on. Simple as that — almost.

Some actors getting comfortable with three-camera shooting may be noticing the red lights out of their peripheral vision *too* much. If the director senses that they are "letting down" when they know they're not on camera, he'll just turn all of the camera lights off. So, they end up having to act all the way through the scene anyway.

As parting words to this chapter, I'll just remind you once again to stand up straight. Does shooting with three cameras exaggerate flaws, weight, and posture like the others? Yes — three times as much!

CHAPTER FIVE — SUMMARY

There's a vast difference between shooting with three cameras and shooting with one. An actor's technical awareness is also quite different. Even though soaps and sitcoms are both shot with three cameras, that's where the similarities end.

Since camera and editing cues are taken from the actor's movement and dialogue, it's extremely important to duplicate the performance you gave in rehearsal and camera blocking.

"Consistency" is a word that will make you very popular with your film crew.

CHAPTER 6

INTO THE LENS

We're beginning to get a glimpse of the various types of work that takes place in front of a camera. It's all "show biz," it's all performing, but the techniques used are quite varied.

Looking straight into the lens is only done in certain situations. In an entire acting career, you may never be given the direction to actually "look" at the camera. On the other hand, if you do a lot of work as a host or spokesperson you may spend half your life looking into the lens.

If this is done at the wrong time, however, like in a drama, it will jar the viewer right out of the story. This is sometimes referred to as "spiking the lens." (For close-up coverage, you will often be looking *close* but just past the camera. Not *into* it.)

Looking into the lens

Photo courtesy of S. Carlson

When not in the context of a story, speaking directly into the lens is very strong and personal. Commercial spokespeople are looking you right in the eye all the time, talking to you as if you were their old buddy.

Jay Leno, Katie Couric, Regis Philbin, Bryant Gumbel, Oprah, and others are invited into millions of homes daily. Viewers get to "know" them, they miss them when they go on vacation, they rejoice when they come back. They have "friend" status in the minds of millions of viewers who have never met them and never will, but looking right into the lens has the effect of intimacy — and that can be very powerful.

It can also be misconstrued.

I heard the following story years ago. It was attributed to Carol Burnett while her long-running show was still on the air.

One night Carol and her family were sitting down for dinner when the front doorbell rang. Carol answered the door and saw two middle-aged strangers there, saying they were from out of town, taking some tours in L. A. and thought they'd stop by to say hello.

Not knowing quite how to act, Carol tried to be nice and said that they were just sitting down to dinner but thanks anyway.

"Oh, that's all right." the couple said as they walked right past Carol into her house. "We've got nothing to do for a while. We'll just sit down and wait."

Carol couldn't believe this and had to get a little tougher to get them out of her house. As the couple left in a huff, the woman turned back and said, "Well, you certainly are *nicer* on TV!"

Whether that actually happened to Carol or not, it makes the point. These people had "invited" her into their home for years. She was a "friend." In their limited capacity, they felt she should be just as glad to see them as they were to see her.

When you look into the lens and talk to someone, it reads as though you are talking to each person specifically. That is one of the major powers of television.

That is why some game show hosts are thought to be brilliant by their audience when all they really do is read answers to questions off a card. Some newscasters are considered intelligent and worldly-wise, but all they actually do is read information off a teleprompter that we didn't know before (and neither did they).

These people might not have an original thought in their heads, but they are telling us things that we didn't know and they are looking us right in the eye while doing it. To the human psyche, it translates as pretty powerful stuff.

YOUR BEST FRIEND

Okay, we've established that looking into the lens (*down the throat* is another term used sometimes) is felt by the audience as being strong and intimate. As such, it's been discovered over the years that the most effective way to use this intimacy is to treat the camera as an actual person. Talk to it in that same manner. Actually, go a step further; talk to it as though it were your best friend.

The primary instructions in auditioning for commercials are, "We don't want an actor — we don't want an announcer." By that they mean no stereotypes. The big-voiced announcer or artificially sincere actors are out. They want naturalness. Your job as an actor, therefore, is to act like a real person.

NATURAL

Everyone these days wants a natural read "real." The only people who seem to be able to get away with yelling at the camera are evangelists and professional wrestlers. Other than that, pull it in. Remember that the camera is your best friend.

Whether you're hosting or trying to sell something, the attitude should always be one of sharing. Your subtext would be something like:

> "We're having a wonderful time on our game show, come along and join in the fun!"

> "I don't think anything is quite as interesting as the mating habits of the dovetailed dingbat. Spend the next fascinating half hour with us and you'll love every minute."

> "As your closest pal I've got to tell you, Carlson's Bar B Q Sauce is better than anything I've ever tasted in my life! You've got to try it!"

> "I really want to thank you for tuning into my talk show. Not only am I a wonderful, caring, interesting and entertaining person, but I think you are absolutely wonderful for enjoying what I do. So just for you, we have a wonderful show that you will love..."

Not the words, but the attitude. That's what they are all saying to you — and it works! People are attracted to nice people. They're not attracted to phony people. When nice people share things with you, you want to believe them.

When working with the lens, let your natural warmth come out. If you don't have any — well, George Burns once was asked the reason for his success. He thought about it a moment and said "Sincerity." He waited another beat, then added, "When you can fake that, you can fake anything."

You learned in your very first acting class the only thing you can bring to a role (or to the camera) that nobody else can bring... is *you*. Do the show, read the copy, run the game, interview the guest... as *you* would do it.

When you're dealing with the lens you need to be as honest as you can because the camera picks up everything. If you haven't heard the expression "act through your eyes," you have now, and this is the place to do it.

When you look people in the eyes, they know it because they are looking right back into yours — especially on TV or films. It's just a natural occurrence. The eyes are where you tell if people are shifty or not, whether they're telling the truth or not, basically, whether you like them or not.

Moving in for a Close Up

Photo courtesy of S. Carlson

This is the place to *do* something, not *try* to do something. Keep everything as simple and straightforward as possible and the audience will love you for it. Of course, the more you can actually believe what you're saying always helps. The less you alter your real personality for "into the lens" work, the better.

PARAMETERS

We're back to situations now where, once again, you *should* ask the camera operator the size of his picture. Knowing where he's cutting will tell you how much room you have to move around in easily, for one thing. Another is to know how big or little to make your performance.

If he's holding your whole body, you could make your delivery a bit bigger than if he was cutting above your waist.

Since this type of shooting is used frequently in commercials, you also need to know the size of the shot to know how to handle the product. Maybe you'll have to hold it close to you or even in front of you if they are very tight.

If you are to reveal the product, bringing it into the frame, you must know when it is out cleanly and when it is in cleanly.

Sometimes shots feel very uncomfortable but look just fine on tape. What if we're showing everyone a bottle of my famous Carlson's Bar B Q Sauce? When I show it to you naturally it comes to around chest high, but then the director wants to do a tight close-up with me holding my Bar B Q Sauce. In this shot I have to hold the jar practically up to my shoulder to have it in frame.

This feels totally uncomfortable, and I know I'm going to look like a fool when I see it. Surprise! It works. As long as the shot is that tight, it doesn't look unnatural to have most of the jar in the shot, even if it is held that high.

You have to trust your director. Some things feel very awkward but look great on film. Remember, if the shot looks silly they'll never use it. Besides, it will reflect on the director as much as on you and he wants to keep working, too. If the director asks you to give it a try, you've got to go with him.

STARING

It's one thing to look into the lens, it's another to *stare* into the lens. Some people seem to get mesmerized by the camera and once they lock onto it, never let go.

Remember, to your audience, you are looking them in the eye. People are basically comfortable being looked at, but no one is comfortable being *stared* at (especially with a number 4 smile glued on). If one frozen expression goes on too long, it also has a tendency to make what you're saying and doing look artificial because real people just don't act that way.

You have to break it up. Watch in real life how people talk to each other. You will be amazed how little they actually look at each other. They are always acknowledging the other, but nobody stares except in extreme cases. As an actor you may experience those extreme cases, but selling Carlson's Bar B Q sauce is not one of them!

People look out the window, look at their coffee cup as they take a sip, maybe even glance at the people at the next table, all while in the middle of a discussion.

However you do it, you have to break up the stare. We'll get into this more in the chapter on the "Teleprompter" but for now, just be aware of it.

The easiest thing to do is to try to find places in your dialogue that would lend itself to this. Maybe, somewhere in the copy, you mention that you are talking from your office. That's a perfect place to look away for half a second to acknowledge your office (and, yes, a real person would do that).

If you hurt your hand, look down at your hand. If you mention a new shirt, look down at your shirt. If you have to think about something, look away and think. Search for key words and phrases that could prompt you to look away from the camera for just a moment.

And nobody but game show hosts smile broadly all the time. (Actually, the best of them don't do it either.)

Just break it up. Believe me, you will come across much more natural on camera.

WHERE TO FOCUS?
We've mentioned a number of different types of film work. It's interesting that each of these different mediums have different relationships with the camera.

In *one-camera film acting*, you are acting only for the camera.

In *three-camera soaps*, you are acting for three cameras.

In *three-camera sitcoms*, you are acting for three cameras and an audience, but other than timing, you don't really consider the audience.

In *game shows*, you are dealing with looking into the lens of three cameras plus dealing with an audience. Here the audience is your main focus. The cameras are just there so people back home can watch and see what fun you, the contestants and the audience, are having.

In *hosting* a show (like *Entertainment Tonight*), you are dealing with "down the throat" of two cameras and no studio audience.

In *talk shows*, you are dealing with "into the lens" of three cameras and a studio audience and guests. The host's attention is given equally to all. The camera is treated like another member of the audience.

After the chapter on Teleprompters we will deal with the use of cue cards. This becomes very critical with "in the lens" work because you are being watched so closely and carefully. If you are ping-ponging with your eyes to the lens — to the cue cards — back to the lens, you will look shifty-eyed and no one will believe what you're saying.

There are ways to deal with this which we will go into in depth in that chapter.

This is the time to be very aware of every little nuance in look and behavior. Since most "into the lens" work is fairly close, not only does the camera see everything, but it takes a close-up of it!

CHAPTER SIX — SUMMARY

"Into the lens" performing adds an immediacy to the work and creates a unique connection between performer and viewer. Honesty and naturalness are important attributes for this type of filming.

As with other styles of shooting, this also brings its own set of concerns and awareness; dealing with a teleprompter or cue cards, ping-ponging of eyes, staring at the lens, and knowing your shot parameters are some of the main ones.

CHAPTER 7

CLOSE-UPS

The love affair between actors and their close-ups has been legendary and there's good reason for it. In the close-up is where a star is born.

When Humphrey Bogart asked Sam to play it again, it was in a close–up. When Clark Gable told Vivian Leigh that he didn't give a damn, he was in a close-up. When Lauren Bacall reminded Bogart how to whistle — "You just put your lips together... and blow" — it was in a close-up.

As an actor, this is your moment. It's your shot alone and, as such, all eyes will be on you. You don't want to think about that as you're shooting it, of course, but it is worth doing your absolute best for this little shot because if you've got anything going at all in this performance, this is where it's going to show.

The closest you can get to this shot on stage, I would imagine, would be a soliloquy, but even then you are occupying a small portion of a large stage. In film, your face could fill Radio City Music Hall.

Also, remember in film, the audience is not back, removed, looking up at a stage and proscenium. The film audience is on the same level, close, inside the scene with you.

With the camera this "up close & personal" there are a few things to discuss. Some things work, some don't. Let's try to understand this shot a bit better.

FOURTH WALL
Some actors, not that familiar with film, wonder how any of us can act with the camera so close to us. "Isn't it distracting? How can you think?"

First of all, if they're envisioning the camera that close to the actor, it would be for a close-up, and it's not really as hard as it may seem.

Just to clarify one small point, the camera does not *have* to be close to you for a CU. All the cameraman has to do is change lenses. The camera can be located on the other side of the set and still be filling the frame with your head.

They'll do that sometimes in TV if they are running behind schedule. It's a lot quicker to change lenses than to physically reposition the camera. This is another good reason to find out where they are cutting you.

An actor' concentration has to be split. I would estimate it at about 70% devoted to playing the scene, 30% devoted to the technicalities involved. (Did you hit your mark? Where is the camera? Am I lit?)

The 70% devoted to playing the scene, the majority of your concentration, will build an imaginary fourth wall between you and the camera just like you did with the audience on stage. As far as that 70% of you is concerned, the camera, quite simply, isn't there.

Remember that film coverage goes from the outside in so by the time we get to your CU, you've already shot the master in which you've established your performance and are now matching your major movements.

Perhaps you've also shot a two shot. At any rate, by the time we get to your CU, you've done this scene a few times. You should be comfortable with it by now and have a good idea what you have to do in your CU. Although you have to match the movements you made in the master, now is the chance for you to enhance some of the small movements.

Since there is usually no action per se in a CU, you're not going to have to worry about that. In fact, once you get in position and get lit, there's really very little of a technical nature for you to worry about. You can change that ratio to 90% dealing with the scene and 10% technical.

This is the most intimate of shots and requires the most intimate of performances. Build that fourth wall right in front of the camera, get your head totally into what's going on in your scene, and do it.

You don't have to perform quite as much here. The camera (or lens) is so close that innuendoes read very big. Thoughts show. Let the camera discover what you're doing rather than handing it the performance.

We're back to "acting with the eyes" again, here more than any other place. As a general rule, make sure the camera always sees both of your eyes in your CU. Profiles are not nearly as effective unless there is a specific reason for them. (Your director will tell you.)

DO YOU WANT A CU? FREEZE!

As I mentioned earlier, when I first came to Hollywood I knew as much about film as anyone from Wyoming — nothing! I learned a great lesson from a very helpful script lady many years ago and I'll always be grateful to her.

I was shooting a western at Universal where I was supposed to have kidnapped a woman. The scene was around my campfire in the evening. She was tied up by the fire and I was pacing around the periphery of the firelight, looking intently all around to see if we had been followed. I was talking all the while to the tied-up lady, trying to explain to her why I was doing this terrible deed.

We were rehearsing for the master when the director told us to take five while they repositioned the camera. As I walked by the script supervisor she said, "I guess you don't want a close-up."

Of course, I wanted a close-up! I asked her what she meant. It was pretty obvious that I was new to this business so she decided to help me out. I got my first lesson in how coverage fits together and how you sometimes have to think like an editor.

When I was pacing around that campfire, I didn't stop. I was always moving, changing directions, seeking. It seemed to me like that's what I should be doing.

However, if I established in the master that I never stopped, there would be no place for them to cut into a CU. They weren't going to put a tight lens on my face and try to pan with me as I walked around. They'd just stick with the master and let it go at that.

She mentioned that I should stop when I spoke and go back to pacing in-between my chunks of dialogue. (Incidentally, this is one of the few times when it is all right to move on someone else's lines.) That would establish times when I was not moving, that they could cover with a CU.

Well, it made all the difference in the world, just knowing something as simple as that. The scene went beautifully and I found that stopping on my dialogue actually added importance to what I was saying — and I got my close-ups!

Officially, no one is supposed to talk to an actor about his performance, technical or otherwise, except the director. But how are we supposed to learn? This is the only book I know on this subject, and directors certainly don't have time to conduct "Camera Awareness" clinics for their actors. Thank goodness for the souls that take pity on us poor, uninformed actors and share tips like this one.

I never forgot it. (And neither should you.)

MATCHING

This whole chapter is mainly for one-camera shooting since CUs are shot at the same time as the master in three camera. Still, some of the things we're getting into here can aid greatly when going back to reshoot portions of previously shot scenes with three cameras.

As the story on the previous page shows, you're going to be reasonably stationary in your CU. The director will probably want to see motion of some sort at the beginning and perhaps at the end of your CU.

Matching "big action" like running would not do any good in a CU because it would be a blur and they'd never use it anyway. Hinting at the motion will be fine. Probably all you'll need to do is to settle into the shot. Your director will tell you how much he wants.

If you're starting to think like an editor, you might be thinking that your actual performance, after you've matched the physical position you had at the beginning of the master, wouldn't have to be exact throughout, because they'll either use the CU or one of the other shots but not both. Right?

Nice try, but wrong! Many times the editor will cut away from a CU to the master to the two shot, then back to the CU and master again. Regardless, he should always have the option to do that if that's what he feels will make for the best finished scene.

You should still think out your performance for the master, then match during coverage. Your CU will be a bit smaller, but could be more intense because of the closeness. Remember always to act through your eyes because they are what the audience is watching.

CHEATING

Don't be thrown if, when the director moves in for your CU, he asks you to get in a position, or face a direction different from where you were in the master.

He's probably doing it for light or for a more interesting or less busy background. In a CU, the camera is usually so tight, that the BG is a blur. He'll still have you match your actions but which direction you're facing doesn't really make any difference to the camera. What matters is your physical relationship *to* the camera. If it matches for the camera, it will cut well and you'll be pleased with how it ends up. (We'll get more into all this in the chapter on "Editing.")

Another CU "cheat" is when you're involved in a big action sequence and the camera moves in tight on you. Your anxious face and eyes fill the screen as the director talks you through what is going on around you (in the story).

"Over here, there is a huge explosion with a truck overturning and bursting into flames." You "see" it and react to it. "Then a man comes running by with his uniform on fire, three men cover him with blankets and get the fire out just as the bad guys arrive en masse and start taking prisoners." Etc.

You follow his narrative along with your eyes: reacting, maybe shielding your eyes for a second, looking away, looking back in horror. You may have been doing that in an empty sound stage, but when it is all cut together with the action footage, again, you'll be amazed.

OVERLAPPING
We'll get into this more in the chapter on "Sound," but for now you should know that you do not overlap dialogue in CUs. The editor needs a clean audio track to cut on.

Many times in real life as well as in dramatic scenes, people will overlap each other. Someone will cut someone off, or maybe think of something and interrupt. If both actors are excited, they may be talking over each other a lot.

No matter. For the CU, they want your dialogue clean. If the editor wants the overlap, he's got it on the master and the two shot. As a general rule, whether you're on camera or off, there will be no overlapping on anyone's CU.

PING-PONG
When two people are talking, especially a man and a woman, it is natural to scan their whole face; looking from eye to eye, perhaps at their mouth, back to their eyes, etc.

It's natural, but it doesn't work in close-ups (unless it pertains to something previously set up). If the CU is of your face only, the camera cannot see whom you're talking to. The editor will supply that later, but for now, it's just you.

If you look back and forth from one eye to another, all the camera sees are your eyes going back and forth (ping-ponging). It makes you look deceitful, crafty, and awkward to your audience. (Of course, if that fits with your character, use it!)

Lilyan Chauvin, an acting teacher of mine, used to say, "Reality is not theatricality." This is one of those instances. It doesn't matter if you do it normally, or if it's natural to you. It's going to read differently in the camera and that's what we're concerned with. We want it to look normal and natural on film.

Another quick tip, which we'll cover more in the chapter "Love Scenes," is probably the best way to stop ping-ponging. If the scene shows you talking with another person and it's time for your CU, the other actor will be situated next to the camera for off-camera dialogue. Rather than going back and forth, concentrate on the eye closest to the camera.

This will keep your eyes still and give the camera the best shot of you at the same time.

SAVING IT FOR THE CU
Sometimes in stories about old-time actors, they made comments about how they never *really* started acting until their close-up. Well, if you're thinking about ever trying that, here's what can happen.

79

A few months ago I was filming a *Baywatch*. The scene in question was between David Hasselhoff, David Charvet, and me. We shot our master, did a CU of David H., then went in to a two shot of David C. and me. When we finished with that, I got ready to do it all again in my CU. Next thing I knew, they were moving the cameras. The director liked the way the scene worked so well in the two shot that they decided to just go with it. If I'd saved my performance for the CU, what went out on national TV would certainly not have been my best work because they never did shoot the CU.

It happens all the time and you never know when. You do *not* go up to the director at the beginning of the scene and ask him how he is going to cover the scene. To be on the safe side and assure that your best work gets broadcast, do your best in each setup.

Don't be afraid of a close-up, enjoy it! You got into this business to perform, and here you are. This is your moment of truth. This is the time when you can put most of the technicalities of filming aside and concentrate solely on your performance, on getting your thoughts and feelings across. This is where the truth of your performance shows.

Remember not to confuse ease or naturalness with lack of energy. If you have a little case of nerves, let it work for you. Turn the nerves into inner energy and let it come out in your eyes as the truth of your character. It's not that hard to do; just acknowledge the concept, try it, notice how it feels and let it go.

Oh, and don't forget to enjoy yourself.

CHAPTER SEVEN — SUMMARY

The close-up is the most intimate of shots and needs the most delicate, honest performance we can deliver. Building your "fourth wall" is even more necessary here to block out the activity of the set.

It's also important to stop big motion on your dialogue (when possible) if you want a CU. Matching remains critical, as does delivering a clean audio track. No overlapping here.

81

CHAPTER 8

SHARING THE CAMERA

A considerable part of an actor's film character depends on relationships — with whom and how the actor deals with them — which are usually a major component of the plot. As actors, we have to make sure those relationships come across on camera.

Some of the things we will touch on in this chapter have been mentioned previously, but it doesn't hurt to go over the basics a few times. The next time you're on a set, you won't even have to *think* about them — they'll just be there.

Knowing what to expect is the first step in being comfortable in a situation. If you are in a two shot with someone, you know if that's not a part of a larger master, it will become the master and, more than likely, the camera will then take two CUs of you and your partner.

From this obvious assumption you will know that you'll have to match your actions in the tighter shots, so you will have to remember what you're doing. You will also know not to run off at the completion of the two shot because you're going to be needed, either for your own CU or for an off-camera look for your partners.

GROUPS
If you are a part of a group, remember that the coverage will go from the outside in. Become familiar with your physical proximity to the other actors as laid down in the master because that's what you're going to have to match in subsequent tighter shots, as well as whatever action you took.

Paying close attention to blocking and marks is even more important when dealing with a group. It's very easy to get blocked from the camera, to block someone else, to get in someone else's light, or to have that person get in your light.

Remember to have more than one mark. Your web here should consist of a relative position to fellow actors, relative position and "sight line" with the camera, and relative position to something stable (like a couch, chair, or, if you're close to the end of the set, maybe even something off the set like a light stand).

Which awareness is the most important to you depends upon your character's role in this group scene. If you're one of the gang but someone else has the primary focus, it is not necessary for the camera to see both eyes of your face all the time. Your relationship to the other actors would be the most important here. In that case, if the director wants to single you out, he'll do it in a two shot or CU.

If you are the main person in this group, being on your original mark will probably be the most important consideration because the other actors will then take their relative positions from you. If you are on that mark, you will also know that you are lit correctly. Equally as important would be keeping a clear sight line to the camera.

If you can't see the camera, the camera can't see you. Your first priority always is to play the intent of the scene, but it doesn't do much good if you're blocked.

Let the camera into your scene. In acting classes and stage work, you learned about "countering" when a fellow actor joined you on stage, and "opening up" so that even though you were still talking to each other, you let the audience in on it too, and made yourself more visible to them.

Since in film we cover with CUs, opening up isn't that crucial, but it is still a pretty good idea in a master. A three-fourths face is more interesting to the camera than a stark profile unless the director specifically wants full profile. In that case, give it to him. If not, open up ever so little. (It might be as small as using our off-camera trick of just looking in the eye closest to camera or putting your weight on your upstage foot.) The camera is so sensitive, the slightest little thing can make a difference.

UPSTAGING

Someone asked me once if you can upstage someone in film. Well, sure you can, but it's appreciated about as much as when you do it on stage. It's unprofessional and unnecessary. If you are the focus of the scene, you're going to be placed prominently in the frame, lit well, and the camera will probably use you for the focus. If anyone tries to upstage you, they will look like fools and the director will remind them of what they're supposed to be doing in this scene.

If you try to upstage anyone else in the above scenario, it is redundant because the focus of the audience is already on you.

If you're in a more equal two or three shot and someone drifts a little upstage to pull your looks away from the camera, it could very well backfire on him. If this third actor did succeed in pulling your looks more upstage, away from the camera, giving the best camera view to himself, the director may figure that that three shot showed him so well that it won't be necessary to waste the time covering him, but would instead go to CUs of the other two.

The title of this chapter is "Sharing the Camera." You'll find the more honest and giving you are, the more your fellow actors and crew will respond in kind.

85

Basics to keep in mind while sharing the camera are, first of all, *Shadows*. The more people share the scene, the more chances there are that someone is going to end up with a shadow on his face.

Lighting will usually take care of the situation before you start shooting, but problems arise when people start missing their marks by just a hair. With everybody taking relative marks, big problems can arise. By being aware and countering just a little, sometimes you may be able to save the shot. (And again, "What goes around, comes around.")

Another basic to remember that is very important is that of *energy*. As actors, we are natural sponges and have a tendency to soak up what's around us.

I filmed a picture in England a few years ago called *Deadlier Than the Male*. I was the only American in the cast, and did I love London! The only problem was that, after the first couple of weeks, I had to be reminded every other day that I was playing an American in the film. I was soaking up everything English so much that I also started to pick up their accent. I had to consciously force myself not to.

It's very easy to fall prey to something like that, especially if you're working with strong personalities. Mannerisms, expressions, tempos, and *other people's energy* are outrageously easy to be taken on. Like me, you will have to force yourself back to the reality of *your* scene. If you are casual and laid-back but your scene partner is frenetic, know how easy it is to pick up the more excited cadence.

However, if your character is supposed to become riled up also, you can use this same circumstance to help you. You can ride on the other person's energy to help activate you, but if you don't, be aware of the difference and let it go.

No two people's energy is exactly alike, which is a good thing. The more different they are actually helps make scenes more interesting.

Know that it's easy to do, so if you catch yourself picking up someone else's cadence, mannerisms, energy or accent, remind yourself of the reality of what you're doing and get back to being you.

SPECIAL EFFECTS

Since there is virtually no limit to what the technology in this business will make possible, here's a situation that just may occur in a modern acting career.

"Real life" and animation are blending more and more. Technology has made it possible for dinosaurs, monsters, spirits, and other invisible things to very effectively interact with actors on film. Many of these apparitions are added later via computer (in "post"), which means while you're shooting your portion of the scene, you are working with...nothing.

Enough room will be made in the frame to accommodate whatever will eventually end up there, but for the moment you are sharing the camera with a big blank space.

Three things are necessary to have this come off well. The first is for you to simply "pretend" that whatever is supposed to be there *is* there, but you're an actor! You can do that. Hopefully, you'll know what your monster (or whatever) looks like. The way you deal with it will, of course, depend totally on what it is and what it looks like.

The second is to get a definite height indication. This can be difficult to get exact, but we've seen too many Godzilla movies where the actors were looking about four feet short of the monster's head and it just never seemed to work. The technology does exist today, however, so it should end up looking much better.

What you will need to do is to have a definite mark for you to look at. If your invisible monster is moving, have a moving mark set up so you can go back to *exactly* the same place every time. This way, your various takes will all match, plus you'll be able to look at your monster, look away at something else, and return exactly to the same spot, as you would if it were really there.

If it's not feasible to have someone holding something up in the air for you to use as a mark, have the director set where he wants you to look, then find a visual mark like you do for a regular scene. Perhaps the top of an off-stage ladder, or if you're outside, try a tree, an area of a nearby rooftop, etc.

Third, if this invisible something (as in animation to be added later) is talking with you, make sure you have a definite sight mark and that whoever is providing the off-camera lines or sounds does it from the area where you are looking. To react correctly, you need to *hear* your invisible friend's voice coming from where it eventually will be.

In the chapter on sound I'll tell you a story of just how disconcerting it can be when the two don't correspond.

KIDS AND DOGS

Sharing the camera with kids and dogs has it's own unique challenges. Your entire approach to working might have to be altered a bit for these scenes. The director, crew, and everybody will be relying on you more than usual since you will be the responsible one.

No one knows exactly what a kid or a dog will do, so you will have to be steady while also remaining flexible enough to go along with whatever happens. Depending, of course, upon what you're doing, working with a dog is sometimes easier than working with a child because movie dogs are usually better trained. Like we talked about with horses, show a movie dog what he has to do three or four times and usually he'll do it for you again.

Sometimes it's necessary for you to spend some off-camera time getting to know the animal (and getting it to know you) but not always. It depends on your relationship in the picture. If the dog just has to jump in the car or lick your face, that's no problem for these dogs. (One is a simple command, the other is a little honey on your face.)

If the dog is supposed to follow you everywhere or if you have to get in a fight with one or even play roughly with a dog, I'd suggest spending some time with it. The trainers will help you and will never be far away. They're generally right outside the frame ready for anything.

Needless to say, dealing with larger animals like lions, tigers, or bears (oh no!) requires much more time and attention and some serious work with the trainers. A stunt double will do most of the dangerous work, but the director still may want to cut into a CU to help establish that really is you in that bear's clutches, so you still might have to get involved a bit. Sometimes it can get pretty exciting.

<<<<<>>>>>

The main trick in dealing with kids is to keep it fun. Here it pays off in spades if you spend some time with the child and get to know each other. Now's the time to dust off that old magic trick you used to be able to do, or help the kid with his yo-yo. This is always time well spent, especially if you two are supposed to have a good relationship on camera. There is a limit to how much the little ones can "act."

If you are a stranger to this child, he may know all his lines, but love is not going to show in his eyes even if you are supposed to be his favorite parent.

If you've just finished playing with him, though, familiarity shines through and will make for a better, more realistic, warmer scene. The father–son relationship in *Kramer vs. Kramer* with Dustin Hoffman was wonderful, but they had a great relationship off camera as well.

Tom Cruise in *Jerry Maguire* got such a kick out of the little kid appearing with him that it was hard for him to get through some of the scenes without cracking up. That kind of an approach can lead to that kind of a screen relationship. Intimacy on the screen with a child is not going to show unless you've established a degree of that off camera.

Children also have different legalities that everybody has to work around. They can only work so many hours in a day, have to have a teacher on the set, and spend a certain number of hours in school, depending on the age of the child. In addition, they must always be accompanied by a state social worker to make sure that all the rules are abided by. A parent of the child is usually on set as well.

INFANTS

When shooting with infants, films like to cast twins or, if possible, triplets. Since lines aren't involved and they could use any one of them, they'll simply choose the one that isn't crying.

Very seldom will you get to work with an actual newborn, but if you do it's quite an experience.

> *Lesley Ann Warren and I were doing an episode of a series in which we were supposed to be the proud parents of a brand new baby. The baby they got for us was actually three days old, but close enough!*

> *The day of the shoot Lesley and I found out that we were going to have a total of fifteen seconds with the child under the lights. That was it. We started rehearsing, then shot our entire scenes with Lesley holding a doll in such a way that the camera couldn't see it. The real baby would then be established in a close two shot (baby and Lesley) that I would then walk into.*

I've never seen so much tension on a set as that day when everyone was preparing for this upcoming fifteen seconds. When everything was finally lit and ready, the baby arrived in the arms of a registered nurse, mother by the side, with a state social worker leading the way. She immediately went to the director and went over the rules again. Everybody agreed.

Since it takes a few seconds for the cameras to attain full shooting speed, the cameras were started and slated before the baby was brought in. The nurse then carried the baby into the set, placed her in Lesley's arms and ran out. The fifteen seconds began.

Lesley looked down lovingly, and I walked into the shot looking like a proud papa while saying a line or two. As soon as I finished my last line, I quickly ran out of the frame, then did it again. We had just finished our last lines for the second time when the nurse came into the set and took the baby. Our fifteen seconds were over! But, we'd gotten two takes out of it and the kid got her first paycheck at three days old.

And when it all got cut together, you'd swear that baby was there the whole time.

In dealing with kids and dogs, try to stay as focused as possible and be as *patient* as you can possibly be. Believe me, it will be greatly appreciated.

COMMERCIALS

Sharing the camera with other actors in commercials is essentially the same as we've discussed above. The main difference is that you're now also going to be sharing the screen with "The Product." In a commercial, the product is not a prop — it is the *Star*!

The product is what's paying the bills and is the sole reason everybody's there on the commercial set. Here it is excruciatingly important for you to know your frame parameters. The product *must* be placed exactly on its mark, in perfect light and focus, or you must keep trying until you get it exactly right.

Make sure your ego is well informed before starting to film your commercial. If it seems that people are much more concerned with how this jar of Carlson's Bar B Q Sauce looks than how you look — you're right. The jar is the star and you are a supporting player.

Your relationship is akin to Vanna White and her letters — they are the stars, she is the means of delivery. You are the vase holding the flowers, the product is the bouquet.

The fact that you are not the star doesn't mean that your job is easy, far from it. You still have thirty to sixty seconds to make everyone in America love you, love the product more, and want to run out and buy it immediately — and you're to do this using the ad agency's words! Like I said, it's not easy.

HERO
As you are rehearsing your commercial you will be given a jar of Carlson's Bar B Q Sauce to practice with. You will get used to placing it exactly on its mark with the label turned just right so the camera can read it. You'll practice tipping the jar just a little bit this way or that as you bring it in frame, so it won't cause a light flare in the camera or other problems.

When you're all ready, they will call for the "hero jar." With the care devoted to shooting a three-day-old baby, props will bring in the jar of Carlson's Bar B Q Sauce. This is a perfect jar with a perfect label built exclusively for filming this commercial. There may be only one of these hero jars, so great care is taken with it.

Regardless of the commercial, there will always be a hero product. Usually there will be two or three but not always. If it's a credit card shoot, the hero will be without fingerprints or blemishes of any kind. If it's whipping cream, a very well paid, experienced cook will be making pies like crazy and putting the whipping cream on "just so" before every shot, which will then be replaced by yet another because the lights make the whipping cream melt and look soggy. Every product has its own special consideration.

Just remember that it, the product, actually is your boss. Treat it carefully and reverently. Be *proud* to share the camera with it, let those feelings show, and you'll do fine.

CHAPTER EIGHT — SUMMARY

Sharing the camera is primarily about awareness — making sure you are not blocked from the camera or blocking someone else, watching for shadows, and keeping your own energy and character during your work with others.

Kids and dogs need another kind of awareness, basically to keep it as much fun as possible. In commercials, your awareness is on the product. *It* is the star; you are the supporting player.

CHAPTER 9

ACTING FOR THE CAMERA

An actor, to do his best creative work, has to be flexible, especially in film. This is not an acting book. There are many places where you can learn to act. The reason for this book is that, as an actor, there are very few places where you can find out what's going to be expected of you on a film set.

But, we'll also look for correlation's between the acting you've learned for stage and the acting required for film. Creating your character can still be the same as on stage (maybe a little quicker). Giving that character "life," however, is quite a different process.

We've already discussed some of the requirements necessary for effective film acting for various camera configurations. In this chapter we'll put these observations together and add a few more. Our approach here will be to find ways to make this film technology work *for* us as actors.

You're already taking the first step by reading this book. You have to learn as much as you can about what's going on. The more you know, the less intimidated you will be by the process. The less intimidated you are, the more you'll be able to concentrate on the business of acting and the better your film work will be.

If you are new to a set, come early. Get to know the tempo of the shoot (each has its own "personality"). Meet the key players: director, first and second ADs, camera operator, script supervisor, makeup, and wardrobe. (You'll meet most of them before you start shooting anyway.)

As you're soaking up the feeling of the set, start introducing your character into your mind in these circumstances. Start getting your character familiar with these surroundings also. This may sound strange, but think about it. So far, your character may have only known life in your living room. Get him (and you) used to coming out in these settings. After all, it is *here* that your character actually will live.

Even if your part is small, it's good to read the whole script or as much of it as you can. It's important to know where you are in the story, what's happened and what's going to happen. Also, each script has it's own "feel." You want to be a part of that also.

If you're doing an episode of an existing TV series or soap, watching the show can help a lot. This can give you a head start right there as to what kind of performance the director will be after. You'll be able to see what the show's feel and tempo is, as well as become somewhat familiar with the story line and how your character fits into it.

Remember that in film the story will be shot in pieces. Your call sheet will show you what's going to be shot and when so you will know, roughly, what to expect.

It's also a good idea to have as much of your part memorized as possible by the time you get to the set. Things on film sets change constantly, including what's going to be shot. The better prepared you are, the more flexible you'll be and the less you'll be thrown by last minute changes.

You may remember from acting classes along the way, that a "character arc" is the path the character takes, emotionally and intellectually (sometimes even physically), during the script. He may start out a happily married accountant. His wife may leave him and he becomes unhappy. He loses his job and becomes bitter. He gets in a fight, a man dies, and he runs. He is now a fugitive, etc.

Even though it's technically the same person, how that character will act at various points in the situation we've just described is quite different. When shooting out of context, which is 90% of the time, you must be very aware of where you are in this character arc.

It's not only the technical things that have to match. Your emotional levels and your performance have to also.

REAL LIFE

As we discussed in the "One Camera" chapter, acting for film is much more like real life than stage acting. There is no back row to project to and your motions only have to be as big or small as they would be in real life. If the person you're supposed to be talking to in the story is standing three feet away from you, when the scene is filmed the person will still be standing three feet away from you.

Confusion on stage may be shown with an action as big as throwing up your arms in an exaggerated shrug. On camera that same emotion could be shown by a look and the raising of an eyebrow.

Other than the camera awareness we've discussed, you really don't have to perform for the camera. You play the *reality* of the scene, the camera peeks in. The exception, of course, is when you're playing broad comedy. Still, you have to keep the intent of the scene in mind and then...go for it!

ACTING TIP

This might be a good place to throw in a general acting tip for film action. Remember that every move you make has to be captured by the camera and kept within the confines of a sometimes quite small frame in the camera.

Whenever possible, slow your movements down just a bit (such as when getting up out of a chair) and always keep them as steady as you can so as to allow the camera operator to have a better chance of keeping you in the frame.

If it's required of you in the scene to suddenly take off running very fast, fall quickly to the floor, or some such action, rehearse those moves with the camera operator so he will know for sure what you're going to do, when you are going to do it, and how fast.

ENERGY

When you think of "natural" and "ease" in connection with a performance, again, please don't confuse ease with lack of energy.

Energy is the prime ingredient in any character (even if the character is you!). Lack of energy comes out boring on the screen. I'm not saying you have to bounce around the set (actually, I'd prefer you didn't). But, let's see the inner fire!

Filmed and taped stories are built around people who believe fervently in something. There are "big emotions" involved here — love, hate, fear, passion. The bad guy *really* wants to do some serious harm. The good guy *really* wants to stop him. The lovers are really in love, etc.

Lack of energy reads very specifically — i.e., sickness, depression, sadness, hopelessness. Unless those are the feelings you want to convey as part of your character, lose them. Be natural, but be *alive*!

We're back to "acting through the eyes" again. Show the passion, the commitment your character has. If he doesn't — give him some! Make him interesting.

If you're wondering how to act with your eyes, actually all you have to do is be aware of the concept. Visually imagine all this energy you have, all this passion, love, hatred, honesty — whatever it is, flowing right out of your eyes, burrowing into your other actors or into the camera lens and your audience.

Think about it at least once during rehearsal. Realize how it feels to you and take notice of it — then let it go. Add the feeling to your character's makeup, then let it happen on its own.

HONESTY

Although there are many exceptions, in film you will probably be cast in a roll that is somewhat like you. If you are a twenty-five-year old male, you're probably not going to be hired as a forty-five-year old male. (However, because of audience distance and makeup, you could be cast as an older person on stage.)

In film you can usually approach your character from the point of "what would I do under these circumstances?" I'm sure you're not a killer, but your imagination can fill in elaborate feelings that you would probably have if you were.

Realizing what *you* would actually feel, and revealing it in your performance, gives an honesty to your work that film requires. (Remember also, "no person is a villain unto themselves".)

We all know that it's harder to effectively lie to someone who's looking you directly in the eye. What if your face was filling an entire theater screen? Your eyes would be huge! Lying won't do it. This is one of those instances where you don't *try* to do something, you *do* it. During the scene you don't try to *act* like your character, you *become* your character... just for those few moments. That's where your honesty is.

Since film is so close, so intimate, your character's personality is revealed in small, internal, subtle ways. In an attitude, a tone of voice, a look, perhaps a feeling the character doesn't want the other person to know but it shows a little anyway — little, subtle things.

99

It's much easier playing big emotions, and they will be obvious in the script. We don't need to go into those. The director will tell you what he wants. What we're talking about here is working with the reasons *why* the character would be expressing those big emotions. Maybe not the obvious reasons, but the inside, real reasons.

Jack Lemmon said a beautiful line about acting. He said that when he is building a character he doesn't ask what the character *would* do, he asks what the character *could* do. Just this shift in mental focus opens you up to possibilities you never would have thought of otherwise.

One way to check if you are acting is to pay attention to your voice as you are talking regularly. Then notice what happens to your voice when you start running your scene. See how much of a difference there is. Unless there is a big basic difference between you and your character, there shouldn't be any difference at all in your voice!

DISLIKE

Anger or hatred are more "big emotions" that are not particularly difficult to play and are clearly shown in the script. What's more interesting and adds to your depth of character are the little, subtle things you can add to your big emotions.

I remember an actor who played an officer in a military TV series who was not supposed to be a particularly likable guy. He didn't care for other people and *hated* to salute anybody!

The actor developed a little body language mannerism that subtly showed his dislike. Whenever he saluted anyone, he would quickly, seemingly unconsciously, glance diagonally down to one side. It was a fast action, almost a tic, but it was effective. It read clearly on film as internal dislike.

Another subtle way to show dislike is in lack of eye contact. Notice, if you can, how you act next time you're around people you really don't care for. I think you'll find that you look at them very little; hardly ever will you make actual eye contact (unless you're angry and threatening), and your sentences will be shorter.

Pay attention to your actions and body language during various emotions in real life and you'll be surprised at the number of little, subtle things you'll find that can be quite effective in building a screen character.

CRUTCHES

Don't let yourself get in the habit of using "crutches." What I'm referring to here are either props or repeated safe actions. Sure, it might be realistic to be holding a magazine while in a conversation; besides, you won't have to worry about what are you going to do with your hands. Right?

Wrong, unless the magazine has something to do with the scene, or you're trying to show that you are bored with the conversation. Otherwise, it's just distracting, as are most props that actors pick up to fiddle with.

If you're thinking that it's a good way to solve the problem of what to do with your hands, consider this. As a person in real life, have you ever been plagued by what to do with your hands? No. It's just something that happens naturally. We don't *try* to be who we are, we just *are*. Become that familiar with your character.

Consider wondering about your hands as a warning sign. The only people who wonder what to do with their hands are actors who have not yet fit themselves comfortably inside their characters.

Other kinds of crutches that can be equally as distracting are the vocal ones, like "Uh... well... you know... you know what I mean." You might be thinking that they make the character sound more believable since people really do use those vocal crutches.

True, to an extent. Again, you have to be aware of how things are going to look on screen. It comes back to what kind of a character you are building. If he is uneducated, a little slow, uncomfortable in his situation or intimidated by something, then these crutches may be good.

If you're a normal, confident person, at relative ease in his current situation, you don't need crutches. It's also usually the mark of an uncomfortable actor and only results in weakening your character.

If you have trouble getting rid of those vocal habits, try forcing yourself to the letter of the script. If they are written in, use them.

SCRIPT

This might be a good time to discuss the script a bit. Many actors wonder just how much license they can take with the script? How "word for word" do they have to be?

> The answer is — it depends. Different forms have different guidelines. In a *motion picture* millions of dollars were raised because the producers felt this script was worth it. Stars signed on because they felt an association with this story would be good for their careers. With this in mind, wouldn't you consider it a tad presumptuous for you to try to rewrite it on the set? I hope you answered yes, because the producer and director definitely would.

> In a *TV episode*, adherence to the script is important primarily because of time. They have their story, their jokes, their drama that all have to fit between commercials. The script is carefully timed. Additional dialogue from the actors is not only not appreciated, there's no time for it.

102

In *soaps*, the various camera moves and shot selections are based upon certain lines of dialogue. (When Lance says, "I'll pay the rent," camera two moves to a CU, camera three gets a two shot of Lance and Pauline, etc.) Since the director is also editing the show off these camera moves, a lot depends on you getting the dialogue right and hitting your marks. If Lance decided to say something different at that point, it could throw off an awful lot of timings.

In *commercials*, not only do they have extremely tight time restrictions (sixty or thirty seconds), but every word of every script has been gone over exhaustingly by their legal departments to make sure nothing could be misconstrued or could open themselves up for a lawsuit. Changing words in a commercial script is like rewriting the constitution. It doesn't happen very often.

However, in any of the above situations, if you're really having trouble with something or have a great idea you want to share with someone, go to the script supervisor. If she feels what you're saying has merit, she'll pass it on. If it's something very small, sometimes she can okay it ... or not.

It's funny how actors work. They wouldn't think of changing a line in a play and will work diligently to get the script down word perfect, but will have no qualms at all about trying to rewrite a film script as they go.

Nobody appreciates an actor rewriting. Above all, don't cry wolf. If one thing really bothers you, perhaps the script supervisor and/or the director can help you, but after your second or third try at word changes, they'll tell you to sit down and learn the script as you were hired to do.

Best rule of thumb: know your lines, and pick your exceptions carefully.

OVER THE TOP

Occasionally, you will get the direction to play something " the top"! This means to pull out all the stops and play it as "big and broad" as you can. There used to be limits as to how absurd one would go in playing it broad, but after Jim Carrey I think those limits are gone.

One rule is always true; it's much easier to get an actor to tone down a performance than it is to get him to intensify one, or "bring it up." So, if you ever wonder how big to play something — if you are going to err, err on the side of playing it too big. Everyone knows they can always bring you back down.

OFF CAMERA

When you are filming a scene, remember to be aware that the scene isn't over until all the coverage has been shot, printed, and the orders to "move on" have been given. Until then, everyone works… even if some of the shots have you off camera.

If your Master shot is of three of you talking, when the camera moves in for your CU, the two not being shot will be positioned close to the camera, but not in the shot. They will still be necessary because the entire scene will still be played out, just as it will for their CUs … then you will be off camera for them. This way, the looks are the right height and the scene still plays as it should because the same people are doing it; even the sound can be usable from all parties if necessary.

AID AND ABET

Depending on how much of a good guy you want to be, you can even help elicit a better performance out of your co-actors by your off-camera performance. The reason for this is because you are not restricted to doing exactly the same thing that you have done on camera.

Such as… it's your partner's CU. The shot is the reaction shot of her laughing as you spill your wine all over yourself. Well, you're not going be dumping wine all over off camera so you fake it.

What's needed in this CU is for her to laugh. Pretending to spill your wine might not bring a big enough response, but if you made a funny face at the same time (especially if she wasn't expecting it), it might bring a much more spontaneous laugh which would probably look much better on film.

This, by the way, is a very important thing to remember if you are doing off camera for small children. They usually have a short attention span so you have to keep things new. If this is "take 4" on a five-year-old's CU where he is supposed to look interested or curious about something, running through the same old dialogue is probably not going to work.

But, if you were to do the same dialogue and have something behind your back that you've only shown him glimpses of, or a box with something in it that you won't show him … you might end up with the needed curiosity coming across.

Sometimes you have to get a little inventive, but any time, care, and attention you put into helping evoke the necessary emotions, you'll find, is well worth it. The performances will be better, the scene will work better, the actors will appreciate it, and the director will want to work with you again. Not bad for just showing a little consideration, eh?

OFF CAMERA — SOUND
Sometimes, because of all the lights, flags, cutters, and bodies around the camera, the position you should be in to provide the correct look is *taken*! The actor on camera can't even see you. It's a frustrating thing but it happens all the time.

105

If you find yourself in a situation like this, where the actor can't see you, still, get as close as you can to where he's going to be looking and deliver your off-camera dialogue from there.

I didn't realize how important that was until I filmed an episode of Dragnet *a hundred years ago. As you may or may not know, Jack Webb not only starred in but also directed most of the episodes. In order to have the "flat" delivery* Dragnet *became famous for, he didn't want his actors to totally memorize their lines. Instead, he had them read from an "off-camera" teleprompter. He found it was easier to get that "flat" delivery while people were reading.*

When it came time for my CU, covering a scene I had with Mr. Webb, I found myself looking into a teleprompter raised to his height, so when I looked at it, the look would match with the CU to be filmed later of Mr. Webb.

Jack Webb directed CU scenes by looking at a TV monitor he had set up in a corner of the sound stage. That corner happened to be directly behind where I was looking.

At first he asked me if I cared if he did off-camera dialogue for me. I said that was all right, I didn't really need it, but then he decided to do them for me anyway. Cameras rolled — "action" — and I started the scene talking to the teleprompter.

It was everything I could do to stay in character when suddenly his off-camera dialogue was yelled at me from behind me! He hadn't moved! He was still back in his corner.

I suppose he thought he was doing me a favor but I would have much preferred the Script Supervisor reading from behind the 'prompter, where I was supposed to be looking, instead of having the sound come from behind me. It was a strange sensation to be looking and reacting in one direction to a voice coming at me from another.

Take my word for it, even if you can't be seen, having the sound coming from the correct direction helps a lot!

THE CALL SHEET

Let's take a brief aside for a moment here. One way to assure that you will never work for this studio again is to wander off at the wrong time. The AD's. have plenty to do without having to track down actors who are supposed to be shooting, rehearsing, or blocking.

Awareness of three things will assure that that will never happen to you. The first is that, since you now know roughly what coverage to expect, you are not going to leave until it's finished or if the director decides he doesn't need any more coverage and you are dismissed from the set.

The second is that when you have to leave (i.e., to the restroom), be sure to check out with the first or second AD. Tell one of them where you are going. He'll make sure it's all right and as long as he knows where you are, it should be fine.

Third, you should check your *call sheet* (see enclosure). A call sheet is handed out at the end of shooting everyday. It tells in detail what's going to be shot the next day, who's involved, how many pages the scenes are and in what order they'll be shot. It also has all the technical information for the crews on the back, but you don't have to worry about that.

CALL SHEET

"THE RAINMAKER"

Great Benefit Productions, Inc.
Naval Air Station Alameda
Postal Directory Building 11
Alameda, Ca. 94501-5012
Tel. # (510) 864-0580
Fax # (510) 864-2610
Director: Francis Ford Coppola
Executive Producer: Fred Fuchs
Producers: Michael Douglas, Steve Reuther, John Grisham
Co-Producer/ UPM: Georgia Kacandes

CREW CALL: 7:42a   DAY 72 OF 78
Call is Rain or Shine

REHEARSAL: W/N
SHOOTING CALL: 8:45a

**A Courtesy Breakfast Van
will leave the Mariott @ 7:15a**

DAY: Monday
DATE: February 3, 1997

LOCATION: Naval Air Station Alameda
Postal Directory Building 24 - Stage
Prod. Tel # (510) 864-7311

CREW CALL: 7:42a UNLESS OTHERWISE INDICATED

SET	DAY	SCENES	CAST	PAGES	LOCATION
*Int. Courtroom *To Complete	D 31/ Dec	133 Pt./137 Pt. *	1,2,4,5,9,9a, 9b,9c,10,20,	TBA	Stage - Building 24
(Donny Ray's video testimony)		*(Scenes now combined)	21,23,62,KB		Naval Air Station Alameda
Int. Courtroom	D 31/ Dec	139	1,2,4,5,9,9a,	1 5/8	Prod. Tel # (510) 864-7311
(The verdict is read. $50 million in damages)			9b,9c,10,11,20, 21,23,62,KB		
Int. Hallway Outside Judge's Chambers	TBA	Sc. # TBA	1, 9, 10	TBA	
(Meeting in the hallway)					
Int. Courtroom	TBA	Various	1, 2, 9, 10	TBA	
(Complete all coverage on Judge Kipler)					
				Total: 1 5/8 + TBA	

TALENT

CAST AND DAY PLAYERS	ROLE	M/U CALL	SET CALL	REMARKS
1.) MATT DAMON	RUDY BAYLOR	7:42a	8:30a	P.U. @ 7:30a P.U = PICK UP
2.) DANNY DEVITO	DECK SHIFFLET	7:42a	8:30a	P.U. Per Pam Abdy
4.) MARY KAY PLACE	DOT BLACK	7a	8:30a	P.U. @ 6:45a
5.) RED WEST	BUDDY BLACK	7:30a	8:30a	P.U. @ 7:15a
9.) JON VOIGHT	LEO DRUMMOND	7:12a	8:30a	P.U. @ 7a
9A) JUSTIN ASHFORTH	F. FRANK. DONALDSON	7:30a	8:30a	Courtesy P.U. @ 7:15a
9B) MICHAEL KEYS HALL	T & B #1(BOBBY SHAW)	7:30a	8:30a	Report to Location
9C) JAMES CUNNINGHAM	T & B #2 (JM FLOQUET)	7:30a	8:30a	Report to Location
10.) DANNY GLOVER	JUDGE KIPLER	7:30a	8:30a	Report to Location
11.) JOSH TOWER	BEN KANE	W/N	W/N	P.U.@ W/N Recalled as added to Scene
19.) DEAN STOCKWELL	JUDGE HALE	TRAVEL		Travel to San Francisco
20.) RANDALL KING	JACK UNDERHALL	7:30a	8:30a	Report to Location
21.) ALAN WOOLF	KERMIT ALDY	7:42a	8:30a	Report to Location
22.) MICHAEL GIRARDIN	EVERETT LUFKIN	HOLD		
23.) JOHNETTA SHEARER	COURTROOM CLERK	7a	8:30a	Report to Location
26.) VIRGINIA MADSEN	JACKIE LEMANCYZK	TRAVEL		Travel San Francisco to Los Angeles (Sat 2/1)
27.) ROY SCHEIDER	WILFRED KEELEY	TRAVEL		Travel San Francisco to New York (Sat 2/1)
62.) CHRIS GRAY	JURY FOREMAN	7:42a	8:30a	Report to Location
KB) ANASA BRIGGS-GRAVES	KIPLER BAILIFF	7:30a	8:30a	Report to Location
KB) RONNIE DEE BLAIR	KIPLER BAILIFF	7:42a	8:30a	Report to Location
2x) FREDDIE SCIALLA	DECK'S STAND IN	-	7:30a	P.U. @ 7:15a

Note: No forced calls without prior approval from the Production Manager

STAND-INS AND EXTRAS	CALL	SPECIAL INSTRUCTIONS	
9 SIs (Rudy, Dot, Buddy, Drummond, Kipler	7:30a	Park as directed Stage 24	
FFD,T & B 1 & 2,Underhall)		Total # of Extra's: 62 plus 9 Standins	
1 Keeley Double/1 Mrs. Keeley	7a	Park as directed Stage 24	
1 Trent & Brent #3	7:30a	Courtesy P.U. @ 7:45a	
1 Judge Kipler's Court Reporter	7a	Park as directed Stage 24	*All Courtroom BG Dress for D31
12 Great Benefit Trial Jury Members	7:42a	Park as directed Stage 24	
9 Courtroom Visitors	7:42a	Park as directed Stage 24	
1 George Pellrod/ 1 Illustrator	7:42a	Park as directed Stage 24	
3 Journalist/ 3 ND Lawyers	7:42a	Park as directed Stage 24	
20 Additional Courtroom Visitors	7:30a	Park as directed Stage 24	
2 Additional ND Lawyers/ 2 Add. Journalist	7:30a	Park as directed Stage 24	
3 Friends of Donny Ray	7:30a	Park as directed Stage 24	

Call Sheet (Continued)

2 Friends of Rudy Baylor		7:30a	Park as directed Stage 24			
		ADVANCE SHOOTING NOTES				
DATE	**SET**		**SCENE**	**CAST**	**D/N**	**PAGES**
Tues. Feb. 4	Int. Courtroom		A140	Rudy,Deck,Dot,Buddy,	D	4/8
	(Rudy & Dot remain after the verdict as the others file out)			Drummond,FFD,T&B's,Clerk,Bailiffs		
	Int. Courtroom		60 Pt.	Judge Hale	D	TBA
	(Added coverage - Medium CU of Judge Hale)					
	Int. Courtroom		103*	Rudy,Deck,Dot,Drummond,	D	TBA
	(Angle on the jury/ "Jury of our dreams")		*To Complete	FFD,T&B 1&2,Jury Foreman		
	Int. Courtroom		113*	Rudy, Dot, Buddy,	D	TBA
	(Finish Lufkin's testimony)		*To Complete	Drummond,FFD,T&B 1&2		
				Underhall,Aldy,Lufkin		
				Court Clerk,Jury Foreman,Bailiffs		
	Int. Courtroom		119 Pt.*	Rudy, Dot, Buddy,	D	TBA
	(Rudy calls Jack Underhall)		To Complete	Drummond,FFD,T&B 1&2		
				Underhall,Aldy,Lufkin		
				Clerk,Jury Foreman,Bailiffs		
	Int. Courthouse Hallway		A115*	Deck	D	TBA
	(Deck makes a call to keep the phones turned on) *Pg 24 Revised Script Pgs					
	Int. Courthouse Hallway		A112*	Deck	D	TBA
	(Deck calls Bruiser for legal advise)		*Pg 51 Revised Script Pages			

ALL DEPARTMENTS PLEASE NOTE: A LIMITED 1ST UNIT WILL SHOOT ON THURSDAY 2/6 WHILE THE BALANCE OF THE COMPANY WRAPS

CO-PRODUCER/ UPM: **Production Supervisor: Kate Beyda**

Georgia Kacandes   **1st AD: Gary Marcus**

         2nd AD: David Kelley   Oakland Mariott (510) 451-4000   Room 931   Home (707) 875-3030

Approved by: **2nd 2nd AD: Michael Floquet**   (415) 324-8687   KP,

At the top will be listed what sets are going to be used, a brief description of the scene to be shot there, the scene numbers, how many pages long each scene is, and where the set is located.

The cast needed for each scene is also listed — as numbers.

In the middle of the call sheet is a list of the cast, what role they are playing as well as what their call time is for makeup and wardrobe, and what time they will then be expected on the set.

Be particularly aware of your call times and makeup times. (You may get a call that would read, makeup 7:30 a.m., set 8:00 a.m.) Promptness cannot be stressed enough. Keeping a full crew on a set costs thousands of dollars every hour. Having to wait any portion of that for an overdue actor is certainly not going to endear you to anyone.

You will notice to the far left of each cast member's name is a number. The number assigned each cast member stays the same throughout the shoot. You may be #5. A week into the project, you may be the only actor needed that day. The call sheet will still have you listed as #5.

Going back to the scene descriptions at the top, you can tell at a glance by looking at the scenes and numbers what scene they expect to be shooting that day, whether you're in them or not, and in what order.

View this as an estimate of how the day's shooting will go. I say "estimate" because everything is subject to change. You may see that you are supposed to be shooting in the first two scenes, not in the third, but back in the forth. Before you leave the set, after finishing your second scene, be sure to ask the 1st AD or the director if they are still following the call sheet. *Make sure* you are not shooting in their next setup.

Even if they change their minds and decide to jump ahead to your scene anyway (which happens all the time), you will be covered because you checked and were told you weren't needed. If you're not there then, it's not your fault because you had acted responsibly. In fact, if you get back to the set quickly, they will appreciate it and thank you because they know it was supposed to be your time off.

At the bottom is an estimate of what will be shot the following day.

Arrive at the set a little early, be aware, let one of the AD's know before you leave the set, double-check to make sure you're not working before you do leave — and you should never have a logistical problem your entire career. (Incidentally, call sheets are used primarily on theatrical shoots. Very seldom, if ever, will you find them used in commercials.)

COMMERCIALS

The key words to acting in commercials are *likability*, *identifiability*, *approachability*, and *trustworthiness*. As we've discussed, the product is the star. Your job, in the final analyses, is to sell that product. Besides doing a convincing job on the dialogue, you also sell the product by your image.

You have less than a minute to make the viewers think that you are a wonderful person. If they don't like you, they're not going to buy the product. They won't buy the product if they don't identify with you. Nor will they if they consider you aloof and unapproachable; and they're certainly not going to do anything at all if they feel they can't trust you.

The reason why advertisers put people in their ads at all is to give viewers someone to identify with. "If these great-looking, nice, successful people all use Carlson's Bar B Q Sauce, then I'd better too. Maybe I'll even be considered great-looking, nice, and successful if I use it too." It's a bit of a stretch to think these things rationally, but subconsciously it's not too far-off.

If you're acting in a commercial skit, play the reality of the scene, have your character reflect the four key words, and you'll do just fine.

As a spokesperson for a product, your approach will practically always be as if you are talking to a friend. That casualness, that sincerity is what they want to shine through.

Here's a little spokesperson tip that has served me well over the years. Have you ever noticed how many CEOs are going on the air talking about their company's products? The reason is because they are *so* convincing. To be a CEO in the first place, the person would have to be reasonably intelligent, have good speaking and "people" skills and absolutely, totally believe in the product and be proud of it.

They are confident enough of the product to link their name and reputations on the knowledge that you are going to love it once you try it. That feeling comes through the screen and makes them very effective spokespeople.

The tip is — think that way. Face the copy as if this were *your* company. Be glad to have the opportunity to share this information with the viewers, knowing their lives will be all the better for it... and let a little touch of pride in the product creep out.

This makes for a good, strong, confident read that advertisers like a lot!

For more information on commercials, let me draw your attention to my book *The Commercial Actors Guide: All You Need to Start, Build, and Maintain a Career* (published by Heinemann, 2005).

CHAPTER NINE — SUMMARY

The camera, wonderful invention that it is, still has its limitations. The more we know what they are, the more we can work *with* it and maximize our performance.

Key words here are *energy*, *honesty*, and *flexibility*. Also try to avoid crutches all you can.

Remember, because of the intimacy of the camera, hence the closeness of the audience (viewer), a film performance is much more natural and lifelike than a stage performance.

The scene isn't over until all the coverage has been successfully shot. Your presence and a full performance is required of you whether off camera or on. The director will help position you to get the best look for the on-camera actor.

CHAPTER 10

LOVE SCENES

Picture this: The actor and actress are in their places on the set. They've been shooting all day; they're tired. The set has been filled with light all day and is about 105 degrees. The two are in an embrace on the sofa. The camera has moved in and is about three feet away from them. The operator and first camera assistant are riding the dolly. The director and DP stand next to the camera. The entire film crew stands watching behind them.

The makeup person continually runs onto the set to wipe them down and powder them after each rehearsal because they are sweating so much from the heat. The actress has so much lip gloss on (so they won't stick when they kiss) that he practically slides off her lips. Okay, everybody's ready. *These people are now supposed to do a LOVE scene?*

Sounds romantic, doesn't it? But that's actually what the situation is like. How, you may ask, could anyone do a love scene with all that going on? The answer is the same way you do any other scene.

When you're looking at the shooting process from the outside, such as the description I just gave, it seems that the actors are in such a "fishbowl" they'd be embarrassed, uncomfortable, and totally unable to do something as intimate as a love scene.

However, if you go inside the scene and look at the same thing from the actors' POV, it's business as usual. During rehearsal they are aware of where their hands go in the embrace, where the camera is going to be, and what they are supposed to do. Believe it or not, you become so used to makeup and wardrobe running into the scene patting and adjusting, sometimes you are not even aware that they've been there.

113

Besides, what they're doing is one less thing you have to worry about. Wardrobe will make sure the strap on your gown won't fall down; you deal with the scene. Makeup will make sure neither of you are sweating mascara so when you embrace, makeup doesn't come off on each other. You don't have to worry about it; you can concentrate on the scene.

As for all the people behind the camera... remember the "fourth wall"? Well, after about the second rehearsal, the wall's in place and is made of bricks. The actor's world now is about three feet square. His love is in his arms. She loves him back. All's well with the world.

And, oh yes, the camera just happens to be "peeking in." Actually, that's a good way to consider the camera in a scene like this. Just let it "eavesdrop." The performances are usually so intimate it's even hard to "cheat" toward the camera. Let the camera come to you. As you rehearse, the director and DP will find a way for the camera to capture what you are doing. Again, one more thing you don't have to worry about. Do the scene, be consistent, and they'll find a way to film it.

The actors' performances are done at the same level a "real" love scene would be done. They speak to each other in whispers. Their range of movements are small, intimate. The actors have encapsulated them-selves in this moment. The camera is so close, blinking becomes a major movement. A slight smile at the side of the mouth can be read as satisfaction.

But the audience is watching the eyes. Sure, they will scan the two faces from time to time, but they will always return to the eyes. This, per-haps more than at any other time, is where the intensity and honesty of the scene are played through the eyes.

The performances are internal, definitely not forced. The scene's intensity and integrity are maintained at all times by both actors regardless of who is speaking, because both faces are filling the screen together most of the time. There may be ECU coverage on both, but a tight, two shot master of the scene will probably be the shot used most.

EMBRACES

There are a few logistical problems inherent in embraces: Should your arms be high or low? How can you hold the other person and still be in your light? And the main question, who is going to be upstage?

If you consider two actors in profile who then embrace, one is going to be on the camera side while one will be hidden. The director will tell you who he wants downstage, but usually the "sense of the scene" will dictate that.

If your partner has dialogue in the embrace and you don't, expect to be upstage for a moment. If you both have dialogue while staying in the embrace, fret not; they'll cover you in a CU. (If it's a quick embrace, they may dismiss with the CU because you wouldn't be in it long enough.)

Another approach they may take, especially if it's an embrace while standing, is to have the camera dolly around your embrace so it may start out on your partner, move around and get your reaction on camera in the same shot.

To accomplish the same thing in a different way, the director may want to have you turn (pivot) your embrace to reveal you to the camera that way. This works just as well. Remember to stay flexible.

One fact of life that occurs in love scenes is that every once in a while you are doing an intimate scene with someone you may not know at

115

all. Perhaps you just met on the set that morning. And now you have to act like you *love* each other? How hard is that?

Well, there's no doubt about it, the more familiar and comfortable you are with each other, the easier it is to get an intimate performance. A good thing to do here is the same thing we did with kids and dogs — try to get to know each other quickly.

Go to breakfast together, get your makeup done at the same time in adjoining chairs, or talk to each other while the other gets made up. Get to know each other. Every little bit does help.

But the main thing you have to do in a situation like this, when it comes to shooting (and even rehearsing), is to realize that you are not in love with the other actress; your *character* is in love with her *character*! Personal ease with each other can help, but it's not necessary if you think through the eyes and mind of your character.

Many scenes in film have one dominant person. Love scenes are about as even as you can get. Even if one person has all the lines, in a shot this tight, reactions read as big as the lines do.

In love scenes, please remember that word "sharing." This is not an acting competition. No one is going to view her CU being better than your CU, or vice versa. Either the scene works or it doesn't. You sink or swim together. The more you can honestly work *as a couple*, the better the scene will be.

TECHNICALITIES
As with any other setup, the actors have to be aware of certain technicalities. The first, of course, is the camera. Notice its movements and changes during rehearsal so it won't throw you during your performance. The fewer surprises there are make it easier to block everything out and construct your fourth wall.

Matching, as always, is a concern since the coverage will probably be a master (large enough to show the room or location where you are), a two-shot which will serve as a "tight master" of the love scene itself, then CUs and maybe even ECUs, depending on how quiet and intimate the scene is.

When exactly did you kiss? On what line did you brush the hair back from her face? Was your arm closer to her shoulder or her waist? Everything still has to match. If it doesn't, as they cut in from one shot to another, your hand will seem to jump. Actually, the editor would never use it for that reason. He might be stuck using the two-shot the whole time because of that.

"Shadows" become a real problem when you're acting four inches apart. A certain amount is going to be natural, of course. In rehearsal, pay attention to the shot the director wants. See how many shadows he can live with, what he considers to be natural, and then try to duplicate that in the shot.

Since eyes become so very important in love scenes, be sure to let your emotions show in your eyes. Perhaps your natural instinct is to softly scan your lover's face, but a tight CU might not be the place to do it. (Again, watch your matching and think out your performance before the master.)

Remember the ping-pong effect of going from eye to eye. That can be much too distracting in a close, intimate scene like this besides making you look untrustworthy. This is definitely the place to remember our little trick of looking into the eye closest to the camera. You will be amazed at how well that works.

When you are supplying an off camera look for your partner's CU, be as supportive as you can. The director will place you where the look will be right, then get as close to the lens as possible. This will give them the best look while still not looking into the lens. You don't want that. You just want "close."

117

Stay in character off camera for your partner and give them the courtesy of a full performance, just as you will expect from them when it's time for *your* CU.

ROMANTIC

In a love scene, you want to appear romantic and sexy, so let's look at a couple of things that will help — and a couple that will ruin the mood entirely.

The first thing to notice in a love scene is the tempo. Everything gets slower. Imagine a quiet, intimate love scene with someone talking really fast. Doesn't work, does it? Even if your natural speaking tempo is fast, slow it down for this scene.

Another mood breaker is the actor who has his hands constantly in motion. Now, maybe this is what he thinks is sexy; he's rubbing her back, then her shoulders, then back to the back until he finds a place where he stays awhile, rubbing this one place.

Maybe his wife or girlfriend loves it in real life, but on camera it's going to look like he's all over the place, groping and nervous. Here, too, slow it down. Give her a man with a "slow hand." And keep big movements to a minimum (if you need them at all). This will photograph much sexier and make you appear much more romantic.

If it's a comedy love scene or you're supposed to be a klutz, just reverse everything I said. That'll do it for you.

KISSES

Screen kisses carry many of the same logistical problems of screen embraces. It's hard to hold both people in the kiss at the same time so, again, there will be someone upstage, and someone down. The director will tell you how he wants you to play it. Very few directors will actually tell you what kind of kiss they want, however, so let's look at that.

The way you kiss is going to affect how your character is perceived. You could emerge from a kiss as a sexy devil or a prude or gross or nervous. You can tell a lot about people by the way they kiss.

Regardless of how you kiss in real life, realize how the kiss will look on screen. Here are some extremes.

TIGHT-LIPPED — This is generally a pretty unsexy kiss. You would expect to see family members kissing like this, or older people (sixty and over), kids (maybe someone's first kiss?), or someone stereotypically prudish (like a librarian). (If you want to show another side to your librarian, keep reading.)

SAY "AHHHHH" — Some people actually try to kiss with their mouth wide open. On film this looks like "The Kiss That Ate Cleveland." If you want to appear as a legitimately sexy person, watch out for this one. If you want to appear as an overexcited teenager who hasn't quite figured out what to do about it yet, this may be the kiss for you. Other than that, or for some other *broad* character, I'd give it a miss.

TONGUES — This is something else that can be used for character building. Too much tongue simply appears gross on camera (but imagine your pristine librarian kissing this way?). Again, it's a very teenage thing to do but not if you're playing a sincere, sensitive teenager — this guy will control himself a little more. If you're a rowdy, go-for-it kind of maniac — use it.

A *little* tongue, however, does usually come across as sexy. Don't "present" it. Let the camera "accidentally" catch a quick glimpse.

IDEAL — The ideal romantic screen kiss for most ages is with the mouth slightly open and the lips very soft. If you want to add a little sexiness to your romantic scene, add just a touch of tongue. You will also find that the slower you do most anything

119

in a love scene, the sexier and more romantic it will translate to the screen.

Use, of course, your natural amorous instincts as the bases to build your character's romantic life. But, also, be as critical as you can. What works great in your apartment might not be right for your screen character. Take your time, think it out, and get the right kiss for the part.

NUDITY

Although I'll direct this section primarily to women, the same rights and privileges extend to both sexes. There is much more male nudity in films now than there ever was, but since film crews are still primarily male, ladies, justifiably, feel more vulnerable. Regardless, there are certain things you should know about film nudity.

The first is, if there is to be any degree of nudity in the film, you have to be told that before you even audition. If you're already shooting something and this is sprung on you, don't go for it unless you want to. Since this is firmly against Screen Actors Guild (SAG) rules, there is no pressure on you to accept this proposal. To try to spring nudity on you as a last minute idea is also highly unethical, and I'd suggest getting your agent on the phone.

If, after hearing (up front) that there is nudity involved, and you're still interested, there are a few things you should then find out.

How reputable is this company? Is this a major studio with a professional film crew? Is nudity really necessary for the film, or is this just something the director would like to throw in to spice it up a bit? What is the actual nude *scene* about? What would you be doing?

A basic fundamental when nudity is involved is to make sure whom you are dealing with and proceed only after you and your agent are satisfied that you're dealing with a legitimate, established organization.

Partial nudity usually means breasts and/or perhaps a full back shot. Full nudity is exactly what it says.

Still, being revealed fully nude as you walk past a window is totally different than being involved in a rape scene or full sex scene. You should be told up front exactly what would be required of you and why. If you agree to do the scene as described to you, you are not required to do anything more.

Sometimes, a certain degree of nudity is required in a film, and, as an actress, you may want to do the part. That doesn't mean that you're necessarily comfortable about doing it. There are, however, a few things you can do, to make yourself as comfortable as possible.

If you would like to have your agent come on the set that day to make sure the guidelines of your agreement are kept, you can do that.

You also have the right to have the set cleared of all unnecessary personnel. That means everybody but the immediate camera crew, the director, script, DP, sound, and maybe a grip. Everyone else, especially any "onlookers" have to leave. That usually makes it a little more comfortable right there.

Yes, body makeup usually is necessary. Don't feel it's a ploy by someone. Skin is a major reflector of light, and body makeup tones it down considerably. There is no rule, however, saying that a man has to put it on. If that is the situation and that bothers you, you can request that a woman put it on for you.

Again, the primary rule is to make yourself comfortable. With a legitimate production company, you will find that they know and understand how difficult it could be for you and will do everything they can to make it as easy as possible. If you have a lot of unanswered questions or get the feeling that the people are not working with you, I'd let it go.

CHAPTER TEN — SUMMARY

As charming as love on the screen seems, getting it there requires a lot of technical awareness: i.e., shadows, blocking each other, tempo, matching, and "acting through the eyes."

Know that a contributing factor to your character can and will be determined by how you kiss. Love scenes are definitely not one-kiss-fits-all situations.

Always remember that you have many rights when it comes to nudity, foremost among them to make things as comfortable as you can for yourself.

CHAPTER 11

EDITING

It's important for an actor to know what he's doing — and why he's doing it. As an actor, you should have a good idea of how the editor puts together all the scenes and scene fragments into one continuous, smooth, exciting film.

This is not going to be a chapter on how to be an editor. It's not necessary to know exactly 'how' he does it, just that he does it... besides, I'm not qualified. I'm an actor just like you, remember? An editor is a master of a totally different set of abilities. Just another of the very qualified, highly trained personnel that are all a part of this mosaic called filmmaking.

Years ago, editors used to have long strips of film labeled and hanging all around their small offices. On these strips were the scenes and the various coverage.

As soon as the director finished shooting the film, a copy was (and still is) made of everything he "printed." This copy was what the editor worked with to do his "rough cut." Since there was (and *is*) only one original negative, it was guarded like gold.

Here's an example of the extent to which a director will go to care for his negative. A few years ago in London, the director Stanley Kubrick was editing his movie *A Clockwork Orange* and was appalled one day when he saw that in the copying process a frame of his original had been scratched by the film lab he was using.

Within an hour, the raw footage had been packed up and was being transported to another lab on the other side of London. Not only did he not take any chances with the first lab scratching anything else, he also took no chances with the London traffic.

He transported the film across London in what's known to policemen as "the turtle." Mr. Kubrick was in one car with the film. Another car was in front, one in back and one on either side. All five cars were ushered across London by a police escort.

A little overkill perhaps, but without the original negatives in perfect shape, there was no picture — and that was a possibility Mr. Kubrick would not consider.

The editor of not that many years ago would have had to physically cut the strips, tape them together, and run the splice through a machine called a "Moviola" where he could see how the splice he had just made looked. This would be done over and over hundreds of times until he ended up with a finished picture.

Everything he did would then need the approval of the director and producers, so his work was far from over. Changes would then be made by going back to coverage he didn't use and letting the director and producers see it. Maybe they'd want to try this scene or that, maybe they'd realize he was right all along and go back to the original — an arduous process.

THE EDITOR TODAY

The editor of today still has to have the vision of "the big picture" in his mind, but today everything is computerized and these people are computer wizards. The film negative still has to be protected like gold, but what they do now in many cases is copy everything "printed" onto video tape and "cut" the video tape.

Instantly, the editor can see how various scenes cut together. He can easily change, slide pictures around, fade in, fade out, and do, literally, millions of combinations. Many special effects are also done by computer.

Once the film has been put together, the videotaped copy of the completed film is then turned over to a person with nerves of steel called a "negative cutter." Remember that there is only one original film negative. If anything happens to that original, there can be no replacement.

The negative cutter's job is to duplicate, with the actual film footage, everything that was done on the videotaped computer copy. When he finishes with that, thousands of copies are then made from that negative.

As hi-tech as filmmaking has become, the basis for it all is still the footage. The scenes have to be shot well, the coverage has to complement each other, and the performances have to match. Give the editor that, and he'll do magic.

Today, the editor is a blend of imaginative creativity and technical know-how. He puts the pieces of the film together as one would a puzzle, but he has help.

Few directors would devote as much of their lives to the making of a film as they have to, to then turn their work over to someone else and hope that they can figure out how the director wanted it put together. No. Most directors in their contracts get a "director's cut." What that means is that the director gets a chance to show everyone what he had in mind when he shot the footage in the first place.

Many times this is the version that's released to the public. If it's not accepted as the final version, it is, at least, the base upon which changes or further "tweaking" is applied.

A director can also dictate the final result of the film through the type of footage he gives the editor. Even though *Jurassic Park* was assembled by an editor, it still has Steven Spielberg written all over it. I, personally, can't see him turning his film footage over to someone else to assemble on their own, can you? Needless to say, an ability to work well with other creative types is another necessary attribute of the successful editor today.

THE SCRIPT SUPERVISOR

The editor's representative on the set is the script supervisor. Sometimes referred to as "Continuity" or simply "script", this is the person that makes the "blueprint" for the editor. She times and numbers every shot, records which shots were printed, which weren't, and what (if anything) went wrong with each. (The numbers and letters on the clapboard correspond to the markings in her script, for later translation by the editor.)

She also records how much dialogue was covered in each shot, what kind of shot it was, and whether or not the actor changed any dialogue. If so, she even has what he changed it to.

In her role as "continuity" it is also her responsibility to make sure that you "match." With your help, she'll note which hand you held your glass in, on what line you spilled your wine, and even take a Polaroid of the wine stain so wardrobe can match it later if they need to.

"Script" is also the person you talk to if you need help remembering a line or would like to run lines (if your other actors aren't around), and who can just generally be very helpful.

They are bright, capable people with an excellent overall knowledge of filmmaking and a lot of responsibility. It's their colorfully marked-up script that the editor uses to actually cut the film. Still, as long as you don't overdo it or take advantage, they are also quite accessible to the actor.

HOW DOES IT WORK?
Besides a general knowledge of how a film is constructed, an actor should be able to see how everything fits together. For an example of how a scene could actually be cut, let's go back to our dining couple.

MASTER — Interior restaurant, maitre d' by upstage door.

TWO SHOT — *Man* steps into doorway next to the maitre d', asks if his party has arrived yet. The maitre d' says yes and points out the table.

SINGLE — *Man's* POV of *Woman* sitting alone at a table for two.

TWO SHOT — *Man* thanks maitre d' and starts walking over to the table.

MASTER — Camera *pans* with *Man* as he crosses restaurant and approaches table. As he gets close...

CU — *Woman* looks up, pleased to see *Man.*

CU — *Man* looking down, pleased to see *Woman.*

TWO SHOT (This two shot will now also serve as a *Master* for the scene at the table) — *Man* sits down, picks up menu. *Woman* soon does also.

OVER THE SHOULDER (OTS)/WOMAN — Part of *Man's* head and shoulder shows as does his menu as we see *Woman* looking at him over her menu.

OTS/MAN — Same shot seeing *Man* doing same thing.

TWO SHOT/MASTER — *Man* puts down his menu.

CU — *Man* is laughing, says he's not hungry, just wants to look at her.

CU — *Woman* slowly puts her menu down, flattered, and smiles back at him.

TWO SHOT/MASTER — Widens a bit to a '3 shot' as *Waitress* enters shot and approaches their table. *Man* and *Woman* look up at her.

CU — *Couple's* POV of waitress looking down at them, asking if they'd like a drink.

Even in a simple scene like this, there are a lot of cuts, different angles used, and many places where *matching* is very important.

1. Maitre d' and *man's* positions have to match from master to two shot.

2. The maitre d's point, *man* looking and eventual crossing out of shot, has to be on the correct side of the camera (180 rule) or it would look as though he was walking to the wrong side of the room.

3. *Woman's* position as *man* approaches has to match her position in the master.

4. In both OTS shots, *man* and *woman* have to be holding their menus the same way and at the same height as they did in the two shot/master.

5. As they both put their menus down, they have to make sure they do it they same way, at the same time in his laugh, and to make sure that the menus end up in the same places in their CUs as they did in the master.

6. The *waitress* has to hit her mark by their table as she enters the shot, to assure that the couple's look will indeed be up at her instead of off to one side.

It seems like a lot to be aware of all at one time, doesn't it? Actually, it's not as hard as it seems once you get into it, but you can see, I hope, how important matching is in this process.

If you can just stick to the rules we've already suggested, such as planning your performance out carefully in the master, then duplicating your actions, you'll find that the part of the above that you are responsible for will be taken care of. Just like that.

ACTOR AWARENESS
Now that you know a bit about how it will all cut together, you'll find that your "coverage" makes a lot more sense.

Remember that the editor (and the director) is looking for the scene that fits into the story the best. It may or may not be your best performance. If your performance was terrific but you missed your mark just a little and ended up a little "soft" or blocked some other action the camera should have seen, they'll use another take where you might not have done as well personally, but you hit your mark, making that scene better for the film.

The main thing to be aware of in shooting out of sequence is to remind yourself what happened immediately before the scenes you are about to shoot, as well as what happens afterwards. Know where you are in your character arc and be sure to remember how much your character knows (and *doesn't* know) about the plot at this point.

Knowing where you are in the "big picture" is very important.

FIXING IT IN POST

"No problem, we'll fix it in post," is an expression bandied about a lot, but as an actor, don't rely on it.

What it refers to are the outrageously wonderful things editors and their magic machines can do in postproduction. (Postproduction, incidentally, is anything that takes place after the actual filming is over — like editing, special effects, sound looping, credit rolls, etc.)

And it's true, they can fix an awful lot. Even if they can't fix something, chances are they can, at least, make it a little better. But there is much that cannot be fixed in post.

They can't straighten out dialogue if the actor kept getting the lines wrong. They can't erase shadows. They can't make things match if they don't match and they can't make a bad performance good. (What they can do is cut as much as possible of the bad performance out of the film so it won't bring the film down with it.)

An editor's job is to make the best film he can from what's given him. Unless the actor is also producing, he is not going to have allegiance to any one actor if he is hurting the film. Conversely, the better an actor's performance is, the more he's going to want to use it.

As an actor, that should certainly tell you something!

CHAPTER ELEVEN — SUMMARY

Everything you do as an actor makes much more sense when you know why you are doing it, and how it will be used. Thinking like an editor will put things in perspective and will help you to see the "big picture" — how it all fits together.

The script supervisor is the editor's representative on the set. Her notes serve as the editor's blueprint in cutting together the film. From an editor's POV, we can see even more clearly how important it is to match.

Any questions regarding matching (continuity) should be directed to the script supervisor.

CHAPTER 12

TELEPROMPTER

In my opinion, the Teleprompter is the greatest invention for the actor since the microphone. It allows newscasters to tell you a whole program full of news while glancing occasionally at their notes. Presidents can give hour-long speeches and not miss a point. Hosts can rattle off the most obscure information about a subject and be totally accurate everytime. Infomercial actors can tell you more than you ever wanted to know about the latest, greatest vitamins, without even blinking. And on-camera narrators can talk a full half hour on the habits of the web-footed booby without even checking their notebooks.

The Teleprompter puts the words right in front of us, over the lens!

Teleprompter without hood

Teleprompter with hood

A unit looking like a TV is located below the lens. It contains the dialogue, which is then reflected up upon a piece of clear glass that covers the lens at an angle. The result is that anyone standing in front of the camera can see the dialogue written on that slanted piece of glass covering the lens. The camera, however, looks right through it, not seeing a thing. (The hood keeps glares off the reflecting glass.)

This enables the actor, newscaster, and others to look the audience straight in the eye while getting fed their dialogue at the same time.

Before the Teleprompter, large amounts of dialogue had to be written on cue cards. The main problem with them, of course, was that they couldn't be placed over the lens. The actor's look had to be pulled away from the lens — and it showed.

Did you ever wonder why Bob Hope never looked like he was actually looking at anyone? It's because he wasn't! He was notoriously bad at remembering his lines and he found out early on how "negative" he looked when his eyes bounced back and forth from the cue cards to the lens, or even from the cue cards to his guests, so he chose to keep the look constant. He looked at the cue cards the whole time! It was better than ping-ponging, but it's much better now that he can look the audience in the eyes again.

The first Teleprompters contained a paper roll with the words written on it which was reflected up upon the slanted glass over the lens. This was a major step forward but since it was typed on paper, it was difficult to make changes. After a couple of alterations the Teleprompter paper looked like a marked-up script — difficult to read!

FUNCTION
Everything now is computerized and it's wonderful. Changes can be made instantly, as can the size, style of font, and brightness.

A Teleprompter operator sits nearby, close to the set. He wears earphones that pick up the same sound that the sound man picks up, which is anything you even whisper. He also has a knob (or joystick) that governs the speed at which the words roll by on the 'prompter.

It is still presented as a roll, from top to bottom, because that's been found the easiest for most people to read. A lot of us read a few lines ahead of what we are actually speaking. After a few rehearsals, the operator will get to know the speed at which you read and how far you like to be "led."

The arrow is set where you would like the words you are speaking right then. Personally, I like the arrow set about one-third of the way down from the top. That gives me a chance to comfortably know where I'm going next, which enables me to plan my pauses, or even to look away, and know right where I have to come back to.

Photo courtesy of Jim Estochin Teleprompting

Since I've painted the Teleprompter as such a wonderful thing, you may be wondering why it's not used all the time. Well, as terrific as it is, it's still

Teleprompter with arrow indicator

not right for everything. The main exception is in filming scenes. An "over the lens" 'prompter is no good at all for acting because the last thing you want to do in that case is to look at the lens.

This type of 'prompter is good only for situations where you are looking "down the throat." Even then, there are limitations. Because of its size and weight, if rapid camera movements have to be made, the 'prompter has to come off. The same if the camera has to get into a small, tight area — the 'prompter is just too big.

It's also no good for long shots, when the camera is a distance away, because no one would be able to read it. Nor is it good for big swooping "crane" shots or "handheld" camera shots, again, because of the weight.

But what it *is* good for, it's *great* for. Let's learn how to use it.

REHEARSAL

If you're on a set with a Teleprompter, the first thing you should do is to introduce yourself to the Teleprompter operator. This person will be your best friend by the time you start shooting. If you are going to do a great job on this shoot, you need this person on your side.

The fact that there is a Teleprompter there at all shows that either there are a lot of words or that the copy is difficult. In either case, you have to work together.

The first thing you both have to do is to read through the dialogue to make sure you can read it clearly. It's also good to double-check that the dialogue you became familiar with as you prepared for this shoot, is the same on the 'prompter and that there are no major changes that you haven't been made aware of.

You will decide how far you want to be led and the operator will get a feeling for your reading pace. Sometimes you may want to practice when they are repositioning the camera. You can't ask the camera to stay still while you practice your words, so go to the 'prompter operator himself.

He has a screen with him that shows the same thing as the screen on the camera. You can stand right behind him, practice all you want, and won't be disturbing anyone. Since you're right there, your sound can even be turned off.

And, yes, the operator will rehearse as long or as many times as you want. His *only* function on that set is to help you with this dialogue. Don't be shy about asking him to run it again. You are only asking him to do his job. He'll be happy to.

Many times there will be camera moves while you are also walking and talking. When you practice your moves and timing with the camera, ask to have the 'prompter running also. It's important to rehearse your moves and the dialogue under "shooting conditions." You don't want to be great when you are rehearsing back by the operator's table, then blow it when you get into the set.

Take advantage of every camera rehearsal you can get under these conditions. You can't ask the camera crew to keep running it until you're comfortable so jump at any chance.

There have been times I've seen my stand-in walking my moves for the camera, when I've thanked him and taken my place early because I could also practice the dialogue with the whole crew.

(Note: If you know you are going to be 'prompted, it's not necessary to have the dialogue fully memorized, but remember my motto: be flexible! You never know when they might have to take the 'prompter off for various reasons, making it necessary for you to do at least a good chunk of dialogue from memory. So, the more comfortable you are with your words, the better.)

You can also use the 'prompter to cue you for other things as well. Between lines of dialogue you could have them write in ** RISE** to let you know when you are supposed to get up out of your chair or **LOOK** if the director wants you to look in a certain direction at a certain time. Through the wonders of computers, the operator can do this for you in a manner of seconds. The 'prompter is there to help you. Use it!

Remember that behind those teleprompted words is the lens. Once again, especially if you're moving, it's important to know your shot parameters. Incidentally, if you are standing close to the camera, you will be able to see a hint of the lens through the 'prompter glass. It's not distracting, but it does remind you that it's there.

READING

To be a good actor you should be a good reader. The better silent reader you are, the easier and more natural you will be able to be when reading aloud — and isn't that really what using a Teleprompter lets you do?

The more comfortable you are reading aloud, the more brain power you can put toward your performance. If you have to totally concentrate on getting your words out right, there's not going to be much left over for the presentation.

The Teleprompter will not make you a good reader. However, if you are a good reader, it will assure you a seamless, easy, flowing, and *exact* performance every time. If you're not a good reader and you want to excel in this business, I'm afraid you've got some work to do.

The best way to become a better reader is to read. The more you read the easier it will become for you. The same with reading aloud. Start with text that is fairly easy for you. A good suggestion is to go through magazines and read all the "print" ads out loud. They are usually, fairly short and most have a point or a hook of some sort. In your reading, try to find that hook and make sure it comes across as you read aloud.

The next step that you can do always to keep yourself sharp is to stand, give yourself a focus, like the TV set, and sight-read the newspaper aloud. Not only will this give you practice reading but it will help you start reading a few words ahead of what you're speaking. The easier you can do that, the better the performance level of your read.

Also, practice looking up from the printed page and returning to it. Remember how I asked you to check if there was a difference in your voice between when you were acting and when you were just being yourself? The same thing applies here. There should be no difference in your voice or delivery whether you are reading or speaking naturally. If that's difficult for you to accomplish at this point, you've got some practicing ahead.

Your main point in using a Teleprompter is to have a performance where no one knows you are reading. This is conveyed not only by your ease of reading but by your mannerisms as well. Remember that behind the words is the lens. If you don't take your eyes off the words *ever*, the camera will see it as though you are continually staring into the lens at the audience.

The solution is the same one we discussed in "Into the Lens," and that is to look away now and then. Don't force it or make it look contrived, but look for words or phrases that would lend themselves to getting your face out of the camera for a second (copy permitting, of course).

The most natural and obvious solution, if you are mentioning a product, is to look at it. Whether you are holding it, or whether it's a car parked away from you, glance in its direction. If the weather is mentioned, acknowledge it. If another person is around, acknowledge him or her. The more you look away from the camera, the more natural you will appear... and no one will know you are reading.

There's also no rule that you have to be looking into the camera at the beginning of a scene. If you walk in, or even if you are revealed, you could be looking away, or down "in thought," or off camera at most anything. Memorize the first line and come into the camera during that line (If this fits with the action the director gives you, of course). This can create a very comfortable, natural beginning that also will hide the fact that you are reading.

ECUs

When the camera is at least six feet or more away from you, your eye movement while reading the Teleprompter is nearly imperceptible. However, as the camera moves closer the chances of seeing your eyes go back and forth increase. There are a few things you can do about this.

The first is something I'd suggest anyway. When you are practicing your reading, try moving your eyes very little. Practice reading with your peripheral vision. It's not as hard as it sounds.

Focus on the middle of the page, and see how many words to the left and right of that focus you can make out. At first it may only be a word or two, but even at that, if you were to read the whole page on camera utilizing your peripheral vision, your eyes would be moving much less than they were before.

Another thing you could do is to ask the 'prompter operator to make the words a little smaller and enlarge the margins on each side so that the words are clumped in a strip down the center of the 'prompter, much closer to the lens. If you are very close, the words can be set so they are all shown directly in front of the lens (remember that you can see the lens slightly in back of the words).

If you use your peripheral vision, plus having the words printed out over the lens, your eyes shouldn't move at all. Once again, no one will know you are reading. The more you know the words, the more familiar you are with them, the more freedom you will have in your performance.

Awhile ago, I hosted an Infomercial for Time/Life called the Dick Clark Rock & Roll Era. Dick was on camera about five minutes. I had twenty minutes of seemingly nonstop talking about rock & roll in the fifties. Much of it was filmed in a fifties-type diner where I walked through the aisles, all the time talking about this rock & roll record deal.

An actor that I have known for years came up to me the other day and commented on the show. He was amazed. He couldn't believe that I had memorized all that dialogue. I could have had some fun with him and told him that I just have this incredible memory, but I leveled and told him it was all on 'prompter.

He just nodded. That hadn't even occurred to him.

I liked that little exchange. What that showed me was that he didn't pick up anything in my performance that revealed I was reading. Practice some of the things we've been talking about here and, pretty soon, you too will even be fooling the other actors!

CHAPTER TWELVE — SUMMARY

As marvelous an invention as the Teleprompter is, it still can't do everything. Even with its limitations, it is of extraordinary benefit — especially if you're a good reader. Remember, it can help show how good you are, but it can't make you better than you are.

Not staring at the screen and looking away now and then can help convey the impression that you are not reading.

CHAPTER 13

CUE CARDS

Cue cards were the forerunner of the Teleprompter and are still used in many circumstances. Cue cards are usually white, cardboard sheets with dialogue written on them in Magic Marker. The size depends upon how many words you have and how far away you are from them.

For any given scene, the dialogue will cover at least two to four different cards so someone has to hold them in place and change them at the right time. Although not quite as important to you as the 'prompter operator (since you don't have to be "led" as much), you should meet these people. There are usually at least two.

You should also rehearse with them, not so much for them to get *your* pace, but so you can see how they change the cards, how smooth they are (or aren't) and how distracting it may be. There's nothing like large, flashing, white objects, visible at the corners of your eyes, to distract.

The very first thing you should do after meeting the "card people" is to make sure you can read their writing. Since each card is hand-printed, each is different. Sometimes the card people think more about getting them done quickly than getting them done legibly. Again, their *only* job is to help you with your performance. If you can't read them or would like them larger, ask them to fix it. They may not be real happy about it, but they *will* do it. It's their job.

SCENE USE
Some soaps still use cards in their scenes. The cards should be situated between cameras, close to an actor's eye line. (The distracting thing about them is that whether you are using them or not, they're there.) By knowing they're there and what they are, you can forget about them.

143

The *placement* of cards is very important. This is something you may need to do yourself because even people who have been doing cards for years never seem to quite understand what they're doing from an actor's point of view.

For example, one of the things card people have to look out for is being caught on camera. In a soap situation, where you have three cameras constantly changing position, that can be difficult. Some card handlers' solution to not being caught on camera is to go right under the lens of one of the cameras itself!

Well, they'll never get caught by the camera but, for the actor to use them, we now have to turn and look right at the camera to get our words, making it rather obvious what's going on. Not a great idea, but you'll see card people do it all the time. When you learn what your blocking for the scene is, take a moment and tell "cards" where you want them to be. (Again, their only job is to help you. By your giving them a position, you are actually helping them.)

CUE CARDS AND EYE LINES

In the diagram above you can see how, if actors needed to use the cards, they could get help by simply changing eye focus. They wouldn't have to move their heads, just look over the shoulder of their scene mate, grab the word and change focus back. From the camera placement shown, it would never read to the viewer. If you had to look under any of these cameras for the words, it would show glaringly.

Incidentally, there are freestanding Teleprompters sometimes used in these situations as well. They look like little TVs on stands that can be rolled anywhere you want and left there. They're not as distracting as cards, much easier to work with — and much more expensive.

<<<<<>>>>>

I think it only right that I point out that as a film actor your primary responsibility is to know your lines. (The only exception is when you have copious dialogue to be delivered into the lens.) Most acting situations will not have cards. The sets that do have them are for emergencies only, as in a soap situation where you may have thirty pages of dialogue one day and thirty-five pages the next day. If this goes on long enough, sometime the words are going to get jumbled in your head and you might need a little help.

If you "go up" (forget your words) on a sitcom, they'll just reshoot, but soaps are on such a time constraint (a full hour show everyday!) if cards will help save a scene from having to be reshot, they'll use them.

In the three years I spent on *The Young & the Restless*, one of the joys was getting to know and work with Jeanne Cooper who plays Mrs. Chancellor. Jeanne is the consummate pro. Everybody loves to work with her because she brings so much to the part and is such a solid actor that you end up looking and doing better yourself. (Good actors have that ability.)

Jeanne dealt with pages and pages of dialogue daily and never missed a comma... until one day. She had about three million pages of dialogue and didn't feel well. I was in the middle of shooting a scene with her when she "went up." I could tell from the look in her eyes that she was lost. I don't think she had ever used the cards before in her career so she had no idea where they were placed.

The way she handled it was brilliant. Still in character, she gazed off across the room (actually looking off set for where the cards were), found the cards, got her words, started the dialogue while still looking off (as if she'd mentally isolated her thought), then came slowly back into the set and the scene. You never would have known anything was wrong.

(Here's the brilliant part.) She had tried to disguise the look over to the cards as a pensive look, as a place someone would look while thinking. Later in this same scene, *even when she knew her words*, she reestablished that look again, just to underline it in the audience's mind that that was just what she did while thinking. (Remember, we had just finished rehearsing a number of times. I knew what looks she was going to take, and I'd never seen those before.)

Anyway, I was impressed. Cards do come in handy. They can save the day. It was nice to see a pro like Jeanne think on her feet and get herself out of a jam like that, but for most of us, a little planning ahead, and eye-line placement of the cards will solve the problem much easier.

CLOSE TO LENS

A difficult situation for the actor is when lines that have to be delivered into the lens are put on cue cards. Since the cards cannot be put over the lens, to look at the cards is to look to the side of the lens and it will read that way. If you go back and forth from the cue cards to the lens, we're back to our good old ping-pong effect. Distracting under any situation. What do you do?

Well, there are a few things, but the only good one is to try to get the lines down and just do them without the help of anything. If that can't be done, depending on the dialogue and the situation, sometimes the director can shoot the scene in "pieces" so all you have to learn are a couple of paragraphs at a time.

If you have a director who is willing to work with you, another suggestion could be to move the camera away from you for this shot. He can change lenses and have the camera a few feet farther back from you while still giving the same framing on film. The further away the camera is, even with this type of lens, the less your eye movement will show.

The cards could be held directly to one side of the lens. The card person will raise the card as you read, making sure the line you are speaking is level with the lens. This isn't a perfect solution but, sometimes, it's the best alternative.

Even in this situation, I would look at the cards as close to the lens as possible, read as much as you can with your peripheral vision and hold that look. Even going from that look to "into the lens" and back again will only call attention to the fact that something is going on.

If the camera can't be moved, one more strange approach can be tried. Cut a piece of paper or cardboard a little more than a foot tall and about seven inches wide. In the middle, cut a hole the size of the lens that is on the camera. Print your dialogue in letters as small as you can still read on top and below the lens hole, then slip the card over the lens.

This will bring your look close to the lens. Again, you won't be right on it and even with the best peripheral reading, your looks will still be slightly above the lens and slightly below. (If the dialogue permits, this may be broken up and made less obvious by looking away for a half second. If you are looking slightly above the lens, look away, and come back slightly below the lens, your eye move down will not be as noticeable.)

If you have tons of dialogue to memorize (such as in a soap situation), one thing that will ease the burden a little is to count on the cards for telephone calls. (I'm assuming that by now you can act just as naturally while you are reading as when you are not.) Since people usually gaze off into space while talking on the phone anyway, what's to stop having the cards located right where you happen to be staring off into space? Nothing.

Again, the more you know your words, the better. Even on phone calls, no one looks at one single space the whole time. Look away, look around, be natural, but you can also be crafty and sneak a peek now and then.

Before we leave this, I want to reiterate that these are last-ditch efforts, definitely not to be counted on. Nothing is better than simply knowing and delivering your lines. However, we all know that problems can occur. I'm just sharing some of the creative maneuvers I've experienced to help you possibly minimize an uncomfortable situation. These are not *solutions*, and they certainly don't work in all situations. For emergency use only! Just file them away in the back of your mind and hope you'll never have to use them.

CHAPTER THIRTEEN — SUMMARY

Cue cards are not nearly as effective for "in the lens" use, but can be used quite effectively in a scene. The key here is placement.

Whereas an "over the lens" 'prompter is used to enable an actor to deliver copious amounts of dialogue, cue cards are practically always used for emergencies or auditions.

CHAPTER 14

LIGHT AND **SOUND**

Anyone who has ever taken a snapshot knows how important light is to film. Different types of film require different intensities of light. (Videotape requires even more than film does.)

Much of this book has been dedicated to the importance of "matching." Those in charge of lighting have to be aware of this also. Shooting outside carries its own set of problems with the ever-changing sun, clouds, and other weather conditions. Since the matching required in scene coverage is so precise, there is a difference that has to be compensated for, even between the light at two o'clock in the afternoon and the light at four o'clock in the afternoon.

When you realize that some difficult scenes sometimes take a few days to film, keeping that light constant becomes a monumental task. "Sound stages" were originally created when films went from "silents" to "talkies," but they turned out to be a blessing for the lighting folks also. Here is a place where they can create their own environment… and the light stays the same all day long.

PERSONNEL
Lighting is one of the most important skills in film making. It's one of those things that you don't notice at all when it's done correctly, but is glaringly obvious when it's wrong.

The person who calls the shots here is the Director of Photography. The "mood" and "look" of the film is in his hands. He decides what he wants and relays his vision to the "Gaffer." The gaffer is the head of the lighting crew. His job is to bring the D.P.'s ideas into reality.

The gaffer's main assistant is called the "Best Boy" (even if it's a girl).

Together, with the help of various Grips (if necessary), the gaffer and best boy will physically set up the various lights, situate generators, angle "shiny boards," insert gels, filters, cutters, etc., until the scene is lit the way the D.P. wants it.

MAKEUP

Makeup is actually a side effect of lighting. Especially in the old days when light had to be poured into the set in order to be properly photographed, natural skin tones were wiped out. Skin reflects light very well. Everyone ended up looking like ghosts.

Non-reflective makeup had to be put on to be able to see people at all. Over the years makeup, like most everything else related to film-making, has evolved into an art form. Makeup is still needed to bring out facial features but doesn't have to be caked on like before. It's become much more subtle (except, of course, for gory "slasher" movies.).

SHOOTING OUTSIDE

Earlier, I noted some of the obvious problems to be dealt with while shooting outside. The basic tool the gaffer uses to keep outside sets lit is a board on a stand called, aptly enough, a "shiny board." This board allows the sun to be redirected to the area where they want to it to be, easily and cheaply. It's basically just a large reflector but is the main source of light when shooting outside.

Photo courtesy of Mole-Richardson

Shiny Board

One side of the shiny board is *very* shiny. This side is used when the sun is not very bright and every ray possible has to be gleaned from it, or if they want the set very, very bright. As an actor, you don't want to be in front of one too long. (They get *hot!*)

On the other side is the actor's friend. This side is also shiny but with little "flaps" that dampen and soften the effect of the reflection. This is usually much more comfortable for the actor. You want the scene to be well lit, but you also don't want to be "squinting" into the camera.

I never knew there was such a difference between brown eyes and blue eyes. Lighting personnel know that difference only too well. Quite simply, brown eyes can handle light, blue eyes can't. Being a blue-eyed actor myself, I have had to deal with that uncomfortable reality my entire career. I will be squinting like mad and the brown-eyed actor next to me is wondering what my problem is.

The solution usually is that everybody has to "give" a little. The gaffer will try to get by with a little less light than he would actually prefer and I have to act in a little more light than I would actually be comfortable with. It's times like this when all parties have to remember that our mutual goal is the best-looking film possible... and that doesn't include under-lit sets or squinty actors.

Lighting is another reason to make yourself a nice person to work with. The lighting crew usually can soften focus ever so slightly on most everything to make life in the set much more enjoyable. But, if you've made yourself a total pain to work with... well, you figure it out.

As an actor, your main concern with lighting is to make sure that you are in it. Rehearsal is the time to notice (along with everything else) how the lighting is set up for you and to make sure that the marks you've been given do, in fact, situate you well in your *key light*. (This is the main light responsible for lighting you in this shot. It may change to a different light every shot.)

You may need to become aware of little things. For instance, when you walk into this shot, if you stand primarily on your left leg you will be lit fine, while if you are on your right, you may be out of your light. Sometimes it's that critical. That's why being comfortable with your marks and being able to hit them as precisely as possible is so important.

Another thing that may help is to feel the light. When you are well lit in a scene, or when you walk into your key light, you can actually feel it. It's like stepping out from the shadows into sunlight. Acknowledge that feeling and notice where you are standing exactly when you feel it during rehearsal. That's your mark. That's your spot.

SOUND

Silent movies were great fun and certainly captured the imagination of the audience at the time, but it was the capability of adding recorded sound to the flickering pictures that moved filmmaking into the art form that it is today. Sound, like lighting, is another of the basics that we take for granted, but if it's not done perfectly, its mistakes jump out at us.

Technology has moved sound recording far from the days of hiding huge microphones in conveniently located plants. Today, most everything is recorded digitally and some microphones are as small as a pencil eraser.

There are still some basic, primitive things to be done, however. A mic (yes, that's the way it's spelled) still has to be physically placed in close enough proximity to the actor to "pick up" his voice and it still has to be physically recorded.

The primary method of recording, which has been around for years, is the "boom mic." This is controlled by the mixer's assistant called, aptly enough, the "Boom Operator."

In a large group, there could be a number of boom mics — or not. Booms are really better in smaller, more intimate shots. The closer the camera gets to the actor, the closer the boom mic can get and still be out of the picture.

THE LAVALIERE

Along with the Space Age came computerization, which led to miniaturization, which led to a little invention that solved the sound recorder's problem. It's called the "lavaliere" (because it can be worn behind the lapel, like a flower). This little mic is about the size of a cold capsule and is hidden behind a tie, a fold in a blouse, a shirt collar, a lapel, scarf… any place out of sight but close enough to the actor's mouth to get the sound.

One of the interesting things about being in the business as long as I have, is that I've had the chance to experience first hand the advance of technology over the years. When I first started, there was no such thing as a lavaliere mic so we just had to "project," even if the scene was an intimate one. We all learned to whisper rather loudly but it's better now that we can do the real thing.

Lavalieres of today, besides being small, are also "wireless." A little power pack about the size of a deck of cards, fits into your back pocket or is strapped to your back. This broadcasts your sound to the Mixer who is stationed close by with a receiving unit.

Before that technology was available, we had to be "hard wired," which meant that I was doing a number of romantic scenes with an unromantic cord running down the inside of my pant leg. It then ran along the floor, just below the picture, and plugged into the recorder. Limited movement was possible (as far as I could drag it). Now, they just strap the whole thing on and we can forget about it.

THREE CAMERA

"Three camera" shooting brings special problems for sound. It's not that difficult to hide a microphone from one camera. When you have three, however, that are constantly moving, it becomes a much more difficult job.

Usually, a combination of boom mics and lavalieres are used for sitcoms, but remember, they are all in one set and are shot like a play. There is also plenty of time to "set up" between scenes.

In a soap, they don't have that luxury. There are a lot of people, a lot of sets, and a lot of equipment in use. Trying to "wire" everyone and record them all cleanly would be a major task that would simply take too much time. When you're shooting an entire show every day, you still have to do it well, but you also have to do it *quickly*.

Since at any one given time there is at least one camera holding a "wide shot," the microphones have to be up above the shot line. What's used in this instance, practically exclusively, are the boom mics. For three-camera shooting, the boom mics are mounted on moving platforms which can follow the action of the scene. Since the mics are directional they are constantly pivoted so they are pointing to the person or persons being recorded.

Again, because of the restrictions inherent in shooting with three cameras, the booms can't get as close as they can with one camera so actors have to keep the volume up a bit. If there is any other kind of background hum like a running engine in the scene, the actor also has to remember to speak above it.

PROBLEMS

One of the main sound problems when shooting outside is the wind. Whether it's a boom or a lavaliere, both of these mics are so sensitive that air moving over their surface gets recorded.

There are little foam socks called "wind screens" that fit over the top of them that help a little but usually the actor has to get involved here, too.

The handling of any type of prop can also be a problem if you're not aware of its sound potential. Letting a glass ashtray klunk down hard on a table could knock the mixer's headset off. Needless to say, the recorded sound track would be no good either. Realize that mics are outrageously sensitive. Unless the sound plays a part in the scene, try to make it as inconspicuous as possible.

(However, if someone was to take a *cue* from that crashing ashtray, go for it. Of course, sound will then be ready for it and will have planned accordingly.)

SHOOTING

Like so much involved in the actual shooting of films, after you've been wired and fitted and rehearsed, when it comes time to actually shoot your scene, you should be able to forget all about them. If you have to do any special business for sound, like shield a mic from the wind, you've already practiced that enough times that it is now just a move you make. You really shouldn't have to dwell on it that much when you are actually shooting.

Actually, I think you'll find it won't be a problem. We actors are adaptive sorts and before long, you'll forget all about even having the mic on. (WARNING: You don't want to become *that* comfortable.)

I'm just making a guess here, but I would imagine that you would not want every conversation you have to be broadcast to everybody on the set. (I certainly wouldn't!) If you happen to not care for someone in wardrobe, it might not be necessary to let everyone know that. You also may not want to tell everyone how sexy you think the producer's girl friend is. And so on.

The point is, once you are "wired" you never know for sure who is listening. Many people off set have earphones; the mixer, the boom operator, the teleprompter person, the director, sometimes the script supervisor, and in the case of commercials; the producer and the client. In soaps, any boom mic (even the one close to you) can be punched up "hot" at any time, and everything you say is broadcast to *everyone* in the broadcast booth.

It doesn't take a lot of imagination to see how someone can get in a huge amount of trouble very easily and quickly by forgetting that he still has his mic on.

An aware soundman will sometimes turn off your power pack to save "juice" when he knows it's going to be a while before you start rehearsing again, but you can't count on it. You can ask him to, or later when you get more familiar with everything and everybody, you can even do it yourself. (Let the soundman show you how. These are very expensive little devices. When the soundman shows you himself how to turn it off, he then *knows* that you know, and will feel better about it.)

Best rule of thumb in this department: Be careful what you say. Unless you positively know that you are not broadcasting, assume you are and that everyone is listening.

LOOPING
If dialogue is not recorded cleanly for some reason, *any* reason, it will be "fixed in post." It will be rerecorded in a process called "looping".

I was under contract to Universal Studios for a few years and got a lot of practice at "looping." We did a lot of shooting outside on Universal's back lot which happens to be in the middle of Los Angeles. Between cars, airplanes, sirens, helicopters, and tourists, it was practically impossible to get a clean sound track.

The sound man didn't even try. What he would do is make sure that he got a good "looping track" out of it, which meant that he got it clear enough so that we could hear what was said and the way it was said.

Universal had a rule at the time that *everything* shot outside would be looped. After a few years, we all got pretty good at it.

Looping is done in a separate audio studio designed for that purpose specifically. It's also referred to as the ADR (Automated Dialogue Replacement) stage. Here, the actor, with earphones (or "cans") stands in the middle of a room with a large screen on one wall. The video for the lines needing replacement is shown on that screen. The actors job is to "lip synch" the dialogue; to match it perfectly in timing and intensity.

A few things are put in place here to make this possible. First of all, in the earphones you will hear a series of three "beeps" about a second apart. Get to feel the rhythm of these beeps because where the fourth beep would be is exactly when your dialogue starts. If you start talking at exactly that point, you will start in synch with your lips on the screen.

The picture also helps here because it starts about ten seconds or so before the line to be recorded comes up. Looping, by the way, is usually done a line at a time. It has to be exact, so time is taken to make it that way.

Looping for television is generally done in the way just described. Since a motion picture screen is so much larger than a TV screen, the matching has to be even more precise. For features an additional element is often added. As the beeps start in your earphones and the video is playing out on the screen before you, a white line running from the top of the screen to the bottom will appear at the right side of the screen.

This line will move across the screen to the left, hitting the end of the screen at the exact moment you should begin your dialogue… now take a breath to begin, BEGIN! Take your breath and anticipate while the beeps are going on and the line is traversing the screen so your first word starts exactly as it hits the end. The pulse of the beeps will also lead you to that split second. You will be in synch.

It's really a "rhythm" thing. Duplicating the line you said before is really just a matter of hearing it a few times to get the rhythm of your previous read… and the rhythm of the beeps gets you going. People with any sort of musical ability usually catch on to this quickly but it can be learned by anyone.

Actually, a good way to look at this process is not to be afraid of it, but to view it as a second chance to, perhaps, improve upon your performance! You don't get many opportunities to do that.

Remember also that the technicians in looping do this for a living and are used to helping actors through the process. They'll take care of you.

WILD LINES
Recording "wild lines" is considerably easier than looping. These are sometimes done in the set after principle shooting is over but may also be done in the "looping studio." "Wild lines" are dialogue lines that will probably be off camera in the final cut. Something like calling out for someone. "Hey, Joe!" This causes Joe to turn around and begin the next scene. We don't see the person yelling until "Joe" turns around, which is after the line has already been said, so matching lips is not necessary.

Wild lines are usually done one at a time, repeated three times. You get a chance to listen a few times to what you did when you originally filmed it, then get a few "groups of three" to duplicate it.

MOS

Somewhere along the way you will hear that something is to be shot MOS. That means that what is to be shot will be filmed *without sound*, for example, a POV of someone's look at a painting. Since no people are involved in this particular shot, sound is not necessary. If this is to be cut into a scene, the sound from the scene will be played under this shot.)

How, you may wonder, did something shot silently come to be referred to as MOS? Well, as the story goes... in the early days of "talkies" there was a famous German director who had a very thick accent. His directions for shooting silently were "Vee vill shoot this Mit Out Sound!"

So that's it, Mit Out Sound = MOS.

I don't know if it's true or not but that's the generally accepted fable. In nearly 40 years of acting, that's the only definition I've ever heard.

LIGHTING — SUMMARY

Second only to being in focus, as a technical requirement in filming, is being properly lit. Not only is lighting a physical necessity to shoot in the first place, it also sets the "mood" of the piece.

Marks keep you in the light as well as in focus, and makeup keeps you from looking like Casper the Friendly Actor.

Lighting outside and inside require totally different skills and equipment, making the Gaffer and his crew some of the busiest people in the set... and some of the most indispensable.

SOUND — SUMMARY

The aspect of filmmaking most taken for granted is "sound." However, recording clean, sharp sound while actors are moving, driving, fighting, loving, or otherwise cavorting around is a sensitive, difficult job.

The mixer will come up with the correct mic and the creative ideas for recording but needs the help and awareness of the actor to implement it. If for some reason your dialogue doesn't get recorded clean, you may find yourself rerecording it in looping.

CHAPTER 15

UNIQUE SITUATIONS and POSITIONS

One of the recurring themes thus far in the book has been the importance of being and staying flexible. Making a film is a symphony. There are many solo parts, but the success of the overall project depends upon how well everyone works together.

Much can be anticipated. This book has helped you to become aware of many things you wouldn't have known otherwise, which you now can anticipate, even plan for. Do be aware, however, that practically everyday a situation is going to arise that you *weren't* prepared for.

In this chapter, we'll go over a few things that don't fall under the headings of the previous chapters. Here's a short potpourri of situations that might, and probably will, occur.

"HANDHELD" SHOTS

At times the camera is taken off the dolly or "the sticks" (the tripod) and is handheld by the camera operator. This is usually done in an action situation of some sort where the larger dolly would have been too cumbersome. (A Teleprompter is never involved in handheld shots.)

Photo courtesy of Sea Vid

Video Operator

There's nothing particularly different involved in handheld situations except the "consideration quotient." Most of the cameramen are in pretty good shape but, still, the camera is a heavy item. I'm sure I speak for all operators when I say that they would greatly appreciate doing this shot in two or three takes.

Pay particularly close attention to marks, shadows, and directions. Talk the shot over with the operator to make sure everybody is on the same page and understands each other. If the scene has to be shot more than three times, try to make it not be because of actor error.

STEADICAM

The Steadicam is one of the most unbelievable inventions ever. I've shot with it a number of times and I'm still amazed. It's magic! This is an apparatus worn by a cameraman (a *strong* cameraman) containing a flexible arm which, in turn, holds and supports the camera.

This inventive contraption allows the cameraman to walk, run, climb stairs, and even jump up and down *while the camera hooked to him stays level and smooth!*

Handheld shots without a Steadicam are never as smooth as something that's been "locked off" (such as on a tripod or dolly) but are perfect for high action or achieving a "home movie," erratic, disjointed feel.

Before the Steadicam, in order to have a long, smooth, sweeping shot the crew would have to lay miles of dolly track and roll the camera along it. (That long, sweeping shot even bears the name of a "dolly shot.")

Steadicam® Operator

Steadicam® is a registered trademark of Cinema Products Corp.

Actors would be climbing over dolly track; cameramen were trying to shoot sweeping vistas without getting the tracks in the shot — plus, the track had to be laid absolutely even or the camera would bounce which would ruin the take. There were a lot of difficulties. No more!

With the Steadicam, the totally self-contained cameraman can walk through a crowd of people without even dragging a cord. He can run by the side of runners, go upstairs, out a window and down a ladder — shooting all the time. And the picture he's shooting will come out as smooth as though it were shot on the flattest floor.

(Because of the expense involved, however, you will still be shooting with dollies and dolly track much more than you ever will with a Steadicam.)

When shooting with a Steadicam, however, remember that this apparatus is much heavier than a simple handheld camera. Even though the operators condition themselves for this work, as an actor, take even more time to make sure you and the operator are together on the action to be filmed. What this apparatus can do is wonderful, but it's very hard on the operator. Perhaps he will even run alongside you without the camera to see and rehearse the action firsthand.

It's especially important here to duplicate in the shooting what you've established in rehearsal.

CRANE AND HELICOPTER SHOTS
Most of the shots done with cranes or helicopters are "timing shots." The action begins with the crane or the "chopper" far back, continues as it gets closer, and usually culminates when the crane or the helicopter are at their closest.

With all these big moves going on, consistency of timing and accuracy of hitting your marks become crucial. I cannot stress enough, especially in situations such as these, the importance of asking questions about anything you're not sure of concerning the shot. You should know *definitely* exactly what it is you are to do.

I've mentioned before that if a mistake occurs in a scene, to continue with it anyway until or unless the director yells "Cut!" You can never tell when some part of

Photo courtesy of Chapman Leonard

Crane

the scene may be terrific. In big, expensive shots like these, it's even more important. The helicopter is only going to be kept up in the air as long as it *has* to be. The director will try to make every shot count, so remember to continue your action, no matter what.

EXPLOSIVES AND FIREARMS

If there was ever a time for me to be redundant, now is the time! Timing, consistency, and accuracy are not only necessary to get the shot, in these cases, they are necessary to keep you from getting hurt.

The stuntmen will, of course, do the truly dangerous work, but even if it's just establishing you in a CU, you will still have to be around explosives somewhat and should definitely know what's going on.

Special Effects are in charge of explosions, firearms, and "bullet hits." The effect of a bullet hitting is caused by a little explosive charge called a "squib." If bullets are supposed to hit along the ground like a machine gun, the squibs will be laid out like a string of firecrackers, buried just under the ground. At the predetermined time, the special effects guy (from off the set) will electronically set them off.

If you're involved in such a scene, you can see the importance of timing and accuracy. Your marks will be given you by the director and special effects person, who will also explain what's going to happen, how big the charges are, how close you're going to be to the action, and what you can do to protect yourself. Your eyes are especially vulnerable around explosives.

Although the charges are angled in such a way that they are not going to blow up right in your face (though it may look that way on camera) and all they blow out (usually) are various sized chunks of cork, still, it *is* an explosion. It can sting, smart, bruise and if it happens to catch an open eye, can do serious damage.

These special effects people are experts. If you are in the wrong place, they are not going to fire the charge. They will also tell you how to fall, which way to look, etc. to insure that you'll be as safe as you can. Listen to them closely!

Guns are another area that require attention. Everyone knows that movie guns fire blanks but few know what a blank consists of. In order for it to explode, the shell casing still contains gun powder. It's called a blank because the shell itself is missing, but the powder would pour out of the casing if it wasn't held in with something. It's held in place by a small wad of either paper or wax.

Usually the wad is disintegrated by the explosion, but not always. Remember, *the gun is real!* Sometimes you are shooting a small wad that comes out of the barrel with the same velocity as a shell — more than capable of taking an eye out!

Be careful where you are aiming the gun. If you do have to aim at a face, cheat it upstage six or seven inches. The camera should not read that cheat. If you're supposed to hit the person, aim for where the squibs are, which will usually be on the body, the safest place to situate them.

Most everyone has heard the tragic story of Jon Erik-Hexum, who was playing Russian roulette on the set of his series. Knowing there were only blanks in the gun, he thought nothing of putting it to his head and pulling the trigger. The little wad was blown right through his temple into his brain. He died a few days later.

To try to stop accidents like that from happening, props might only give you your gun right before shooting the scene, then take it back immediately after. Some people like to clown and play around and sometimes it's fun. Around explosives or firearms is definitely not the time or the place.

Usually, the smaller the budget, the more you will have to look out for yourself. The reason for this, of course, is money. The less people, the less money spent. This also means that each person will be responsible for a number of different things, which means problems may not be anticipated quite as well as on a larger shoot.

A case in point came up with me last year when I did a low budget feature in which I ended up getting killed in my car. A bad guy was to drive up alongside while I was stopped at a light, point the gun to my head and fire.

The special effects man set me up to get shot in the side of the neck. Under my shirt collar he placed a flameproof pad, upon which he hooked two squibs. A little pouch of blood was also placed there that would break and seep when the squibs exploded. All this was tucked under my collar and suit coat.

The bad guy was going to aim a little under my face which would protect me a bit and also line up with where the impact was going to be shown. Since the special effects man was going to take his cue to blow the squibs from the firing of the pistol, I was also to turn away at that moment.

His reflexes would give me a fraction of a second, which should be enough to shield my eyes. Almost as an afterthought, I realized that if I turned like that, when the squibs went off, my ear would be right on top of them. I mentioned that to the special effects guy and asked if he had an earplug that I could put way up inside my ear so the camera wouldn't see it. He did have one and said it was a good idea.

Well, I'd go so far as to say that it was a *great* idea. When we did the scene, I was surprised at how loud the squibs were. I'm usually pretty thorough when setting something like this up, but I hadn't noticed that the caliber of the gun that was shooting me was a .45! The squibs were huge!

I was so glad I had put that plug in. Even so my ears rang for two days afterward.

Be prepared, ask questions and know as exactly as you can what's going to happen to you. It could end up saving you from serious consequences.

FILMING IN CARS
Earlier we discussed ways to handle a car if you are driving while the car is being filmed. Here, we look at what happens when you are being filmed inside the car.

There are many different approaches to this situation, but the most common are the following:

Camera Truck

IN STUDIO — They take the door off the driver's side and shoot CUs in a set with a rear screen projection of countryside (or whatever) going by in the BG. This will give the appearance of movement while still being in a controlled environment.

CAMERA TRUCK — This is really the most common because it's the cheapest. The camera truck is rigged for situating the camera on any side, front or back. You just drive along, do your scene, hold a steady speed, and the camera truck will come up alongside and "eavesdrop." Mics can be easily hidden out of sight in the car, and voice contact to the director is always possible because of the walkie-talkie with its speaker on, next to you.

The camera truck is also set up for hooking your car to it so you really don't have to drive. (You do this when someone is going to attack you while you're driving, or something like that — when you don't want the car to *actually* go out of control.)

THE RIG
The most expensive way to go, but also one of the best, is the rig. This is an apparatus that fit on and over the outside of a car, which can hold a camera and even lights. Once the car is outfitted with one of these, you can drive anywhere normally, doing the scene in the exact appropriate surroundings. You don't have to worry about the proximity of a camera truck because there isn't one.

The director is watching what you are doing on a monitor a mile or two away. From there he controls the camera and all the equipment in your car by remote control. Since you also are in voice contact via walkie-talkie, he can direct the scene as you drive. It's quite an outfit.

STUNTS

It seems that every young actor comes to Hollywood with the dream of not only becoming a movie star, but also doing their own stunts. In *non*-show business settings, it seems like a badge of honor. What they'll learn quickly, as I did, is that *in* show business settings, it's not.

Plane rigged for shooting

My first series was a western. I soon found that the stunt guys were great fun and spent a lot of time between scenes with them. Coming from Wyoming, I did all my own riding. I was also young, athletic, and I wanted to do it all.

One day a stunt came up for me where I was supposed to jump from a moving wagon. One of the things I had been doing with the stunt guys was learning how to do just that. As they practiced, they explained to me how to jump, land, roll, etc. Great, I thought. I can do that — and I did.

And then I wondered why all my stuntmen friends weren't as excited for me as I was. After getting the cold shoulder from them, I asked what the problem was. They told me.

The first thing I did wrong, by being a "hotdog," was that I took someone's job away from them. I had just assumed that they got paid by the day or the show like me. No. They get paid by the stunt.

169

Secondly, I jeopardized the entire shot by jeopardizing myself. If a stuntman gets hurt, they get another stuntman. It sounds cold but that's the fact of the matter, and they know that. It's part of their job. If *I* got hurt, it would make all the film they had already shot on me no good. They'd have to recast and go back and reshoot everything at great expense, or delay shooting for a few days until I mended. And it *wasn't* part of my job!

"But, what about Sandra Bullock, Bruce Willis, Stallone, and all the others who say they do their own stunts?" I can hear you asking.

Okay. If you really are pretty athletic and agile, there is a right way to do it. (Except if it's *really* dangerous. The stuntmen are still going to do those, no questions asked, even for the above-mentioned stars.) When the stunt in mind comes up, say that you would like to give it a try but that you'd like a stuntman with you to set it up and to help you if necessary.

This accomplishes a number of things very easily; you will be trained. You will be shown how to do what you're about to do and be able to rehearse it with professional supervision. They'll even show you how best to take advantage of the camera while in the midst of the stunt (remember, this is their business!). You'll look better on camera, the stunt will look better, and you'll have the satisfaction of knowing that you didn't take anyone's job away from them, because the stuntman will still be paid for "running the stunt." Win-win.

Once again, awareness, professionalism, and consideration can save the day.

CHAPTER FIFTEEN — SUMMARY

When the camera is locked off, as with a tripod or dolly, the cameraman has maximum control. There are more opportunities for things to go wrong, however, when both the actors and camera are moving.

Shots with Steadicams, crains, helicopters, special effects, driving, and handheld cameras require maximum attention from both the actor and camera operator. Shots such as these with many variables (and, sometimes, danger) make it mandatory for everyone to pay close attention and work together.

Flexibility, awareness, and teamwork are the keys to success.

CHAPTER 16

AUDITIONING ON CAMERA

It has often been said that the toughest part about the acting profession is getting the job in the first place, and I'm certainly not going to argue that one. By the time you actually have the job, you know what they're looking for, you know what the job entails and have had time to prepare for it, and, additionally, the director and everybody else connected with the shoot is there to help you.

When you audition, you have none of the above. It's largely a great guessing game that you get better at with practice. You'll learn what they're looking for when you get instructions like "nice-casual," "approachable," "young mom," or "upscale" and determine what in your closet will work for these various looks.

Know also that in commercials what the clients are looking for, unless otherwise clearly stated, is usually the stereotype of the category: i.e., young mom — they want Donna Reed; man on vacation — plaid flannel shirt and jeans; businessman — business suit (same for the ladies); a child — they want them all to look like Opie, etc.

I'll be approaching this chapter primarily from a commercial point of view because *all* commercials are cast on videotape in this manner, while very few TV and feature jobs are. There are exceptions, of course, the biggest being "testing." This is sometimes done for large features or when trying for a part in a series or soap. Before they rest a large part of their project on your shoulders, they want to make sure you can handle it.

Hence, the screen test. Since these are usually shot in fully professional sound stages, the same rules that we've been dealing with throughout this whole book apply here as well.

Auditioning for commercials is a totally different thing, however. A little preparation and an idea of what's going to happen may help considerably.

AGENTS

When your agents give you a call letting you know about the audition, get as much information as you can. You're going to be competing against a lot of actors for this role (sometimes, literally, hundreds!) so the more you can be the character as you walk in the audition room, the better. (This is true for theatrical auditions as well.)

Your agents will give you the time, place, address, who you're seeing there, what the product is, and the dress requirements (swimsuit, coat and tie, golfer, etc.). If any of the above is not given, please ask because you do need that information.

You may also want to ask the agents if it's a spokesperson spot or not. If it is, show up a little early because there is usually a chunk of dialogue to deal with. Being early is a good idea anyway because there is, practically always, a situation of some sort that you can rehearse in your mind so you can be more comfortable and at ease during the interview.

(There are usually places where you can step outside or wander the halls to rehearse your dialogue or scene aloud. I recommend it.)

"BEING" THE CHARACTER

It's an amazing thing, but, when I'm on the other side of a casting situation, I can usually tell within the first five seconds after an actor has entered the room whether or not he is right for what I'm looking for. I've asked others who cast all the time about this and they said that happens to them, too. That makes it very important to "be" the character as much as you can when you first walk in the door to the audition.

If you are playing a tough, angry lawyer, don't walk into the room with a big smile on your face trying to get everyone to like you. If you're supposed to be a cowboy, don't wear your Hawaiian shirt. Basically, we're talking common sense here, but how far you want to go to look like the part is up to you.

For formal dress commercials some people will wear a tux to the audition. Others would not be comfortable with that and settle for a blue suit even if they have a tux. On the other hand, I've seen actors show up for auditions in full-flame retardant racing suits for race driver auditions — the same with full ski regalia, etc.

It can be effective. Not only does it show that you can look the part, but might also convey that you have some experience in that area. (Why else would you have ski clothes if you didn't ski?)

The farthest I saw an actor go in this regard was for an audition in which they needed old, grizzled cowboys. The waiting room was filled with old, grizzled cowboy actors. Any one of them could have done the role. One particular actor was getting kidded pretty strongly by his co-actors.

I didn't know why until he was called in. He got up, picked up the *saddle* he had brought with him, threw it over his shoulder, and walked in. Everybody cracked up. Talk about overkill!

However, a couple of months later, I saw the spot on the air and there was the guy with the saddle, playing the old, grizzled cowboy. He had taken a chance and it paid off. He got the part!

How far you go in this direction is up to you. To help make your decision, realize that the clients are seeing sometimes hundreds of people — and they are known for their lack of imagination. If you are supposed to be a businessperson and do a good job in the interview, it shouldn't make any difference that you weren't wearing a suit, should it? They certainly know that you can wear a suit. That shouldn't play into their casting decision at all, should it?

Maybe not — but it does. If someone does just as good as you did in the interview, but *he* looks exactly like the clients want the guy to be in their spot, he'll get the job. With you, they have to use their imagination ever so slightly. With the other guy, they don't have to at all, and that is their preference.

As I mentioned before in discussing commercials, "likability" is probably the most important word of all. Through this commercial, your image will be linked to the client's product. That is a relationship they do not take lightly.

Remember that most of the "reads" they want are low-key, natural, and easy — like talking to an old friend. In an audition situation, come into the room with that easy manner (if it fits the character, of course). You not only want to be the character as far as dress, you want to convey the same *manner* as the character.

THE AUDITION
The way most commercial auditions go is as follows:

Upon arriving at the casting director's office, you will find a sign–in sheet. You will fill in your name, agent, Social Security number, when you arrived, when your call was, and when you left. This is basically for the Screen Actors Guild (SAG) because you get paid if you have to wait for over an hour. It is also used by most casting directors to determine the order in which the actors come into the audition room.

You will also fill out "size cards." In case you get this commercial, they will know all your sizes, as well as how to get in touch with you. Next to the sign-in sheet and size cards you will find the copy (the dialogue), if there is any. If not, there will be a story board nearby which shows in a series of frames what the commercial is about. From this you can see what it is you will soon be asked to do in the audition.

If there is copy, now is the time to get as familiar with it as possible. If it's a two-person scene, perhaps someone else waiting would like to run the lines. (You can always step out into a hall so you won't disturb the other actors.)

When you are called to go into the audition room, what you will generally find is a small, sparse room with a table, a camera on a tripod, and a cameraperson who will also direct you through this first audition. ("Callbacks" are different. We'll get to them later in this chapter.)

The people running these sessions are not directors. They work for the casting director. What they put on tape is going to determine whether or not you get the job, so listen carefully to these people. They have instructions from the client regarding exactly what they are looking for, and that's information you need.

Inside audition room

SPOKESPERSON

If there is dialogue in your spot, such as when acting as a spokesman, it will be next to the camera, written on at least one large white card placed, roughly, around camera height. You will take your place on the taped mark in front of the camera. My suggestion is to start immediately reading the dialogue from the card. These are all handwritten so make sure you can read it.

(If you have trouble reading it, spending as much time with it as possible may help. This is *not* a situation where you can ask the person to rewrite it for you.)

The session person usually has some paperwork to do on each person so this is the perfect time to grab a quick rehearsal. Many times they'll ask you to "try one," if you'd like. Do it! Even if they don't ask, start doing the lines. There's a big difference between running the lines in your head and saying them out loud. Also, if you've gotten fairly comfortable with the lines while you were waiting, you are now preparing to present them (and you) to the camera.

Let's backtrack just a minute here. In our chapter on cue cards, we discussed how difficult it was to take lines from the card located on the side of the camera and look into the camera at the same time. This is a different situation. Actually, it's a much easier situation and I can give you a couple of tips to make it come out just right.

What makes this different is that everybody knows you're auditioning. The clients know you don't know the lines. They know you got them ten minutes before you put this down on tape so they don't expect you to deliver a polished, final performance. But, imagine how impressed they'd be if you *did* deliver a polished, final performance! You'd probably get the job, wouldn't you?

Okay, so our goal is to approach this whole situation in such a way as to give us as close to a polished read as possible, and if we can't do that, to at least make it *look* like it is.

Remember ease, naturalness, and likability. For a commercial interview you usually wait between ten minutes and half an hour. Spend that time getting comfortable and familiar with the dialogue, so you will be comfortable with your presentation of the copy and have a good idea how it should be read by the time you enter the audition room.

What we have to deal with now are major "ping-pong" eyes. These huge cue cards are next to the camera but not necessarily close, so what do you do? The first thing, of course, is to memorize it if you can. Some people have excellent short-term memories and, especially if there isn't a lot of dialogue, can memorize it easily in a few minutes. If you can — do it, then deliver the whole thing right down the throat.

If you can't, here's a little trick that'll make it look like you did. After you've hit on the delivery you want, your next step is to memorize the first and the last line of the copy. This way you can start the spot and finish it by looking straight into the lens, which, you realize, is actually looking the clients in the eye as they watch this tape.

Time permitting, I would also suggest memorizing at least one line out of the middle, which would allow you to deliver one more line straight into the camera.

Also, if you've been practicing your reading and are now reading ahead of what you are speaking, you can start the sentence on the cards and finish it looking into the camera.

Remember, they know you are auditioning, but eyes darting around still make you look untrustworthy even if they know why you are doing it. So don't! Don't be too busy. If you can deliver a natural, friendly, easy read and have your first, last, and middle line that you can give into the lens, you will have shown the client what he is looking for, which is, of course, how you would look on TV actually doing the spot.

This is also the time to dust off another little trick that I told you earlier and that is to look away. Most actors are glued to the cue cards because they want to get every word right. (That's always a good idea but since everyone knows you're reading all this off a card, your manner and performance are much more important right now than being "word perfect.")

179

Since everyone else is glued to the cards, whenever possible don't be. Try to find a reason to look away. If there is something in the script that refers to the weather, the sky, the product, something in the room — use it. Look over at it. Do it easily. It will defeat the purpose if you look away quickly, then visually lunge back to the cards. No sudden movements!

If you can't find a reason to look away, make one up. Somewhere in the middle of the copy, look away in thought, as in trying to think of just the right word, or as in mentally reliving or appreciating something you've just mentioned. Do this easily and naturally.

From the client POV, a person who is that comfortable with the dialogue after only being with it for ten minutes or so comes across as impressive.

A technical note: Decide in the waiting room where you are going to do your "look aways" or your "into the lens" moments, then rehearse them as quickly as possible when you get into the room because you are going to have to look away from this card, then come back to it. Make sure you know the spot your eyes have to come back to. Getting off the cards is not going to pay off for you if you lose your place afterward.

(There are, of course, scripts where it's just not possible to look away, or where it's not appropriate. That's a judgment call for you. These are to be filed away as effective little tricks to be used whenever possible, but not every time.)

In audition scenes with two or more people, everything we've already discussed about filming comes into play here. Remember to keep your mannerisms easy and natural... make sure you can always see the camera... "turn out" a little so the camera can see you better... and really enjoy whatever product is involved.

CALLBACKS

Callbacks are exactly what they sound like. If the clients liked what you did in the first audition, they will "call you back."

Occasionally there will be a client representative at a first audition but very seldom. At the callback *everybody* is there! Generally there is at least one representative from the client, at least one representative from the ad agency, and the director.

This is where you book the commercial. The world of corporate America is a tough one, and many times their job is as secure as their last big decision. Choosing someone to represent their product on national television is a big decision, and nobody in authority is going to trust it to someone they've never met in person.

So, on your callback be prepared to have a group of people present for your performance. Don't try too hard to impress here. Just be friendly and very natural — just be you! This group of people may seem intimidating but they're really not. They want you to be wonderful! They want you to be so good that their bosses will congratulate them for finding you. They want you to take away any doubt as to who should play this role.

They are firmly on your side. Be strong, straightforward, and solid. Be someone they can trust and rely on, and you are going to be booking some jobs.

You really have to concentrate on the director in a callback. His is one of the strongest voices in deciding who gets cast. He is also the one you would be working with if you get the commercial so it's important to develop a good rapport with him as soon as possible. The best way to do that is to *listen* to him. He will tell you what he wants.

Remember that they liked what you did the first time around enough to see you again so use that as the basis of your performance here. Couple that with whatever direction the director gives you and let it go, remembering still not to ping-pong, but to try to give as much into the camera as possible.

The words that are going to get you work are *naturalness* (but with energy), *likability*, and *professional reliability*. They need to know you can and will deliver what they expect of you. Face the callback as a time to convince the clients that they need look no further than you because you are the solution to their problem. You don't do that by being cocky, you do it by being *good*.

AUDITIONING WITH SCRIPTS

Every once in a while, especially if there's a lot of copy, you will be asked to audition on camera while reading from the script. Sometimes they're just too long to put on cards. (These are the types of programs which will be on Teleprompter when you shoot them.)

Your job here is twofold. First, you have to show them that you can handle a lot of copy. Some people are much better at that than others. The edge here goes to the good reader, to the person who can read dialogue with the same ease and inflection as if he were talking to his sister.

Getting as familiar with the copy as possible in the waiting room becomes even more important in these situations.

The second part of your job here is to be seen by the camera. If you look down at the script while you're reading, the camera will have a great shot of the top of your head.

Hold the script up so you can look over the top of it at the camera. Don't cut the bottom of your face off though. Ask the cameraperson how high you can hold the script. They'll give you a height which you then lock in by looking around for "marks" (i.e., the top of the script may line up with the bottom of the camera, or a part on the tripod, or even with a table, etc.).

Try again to read ahead of the words you are speaking so you can deliver at least the ends of some lines into the camera. They want to *see* you. Roll the script as you read it, keeping the lines you are speaking toward the top of the script. This will help keep your face and eyes more visible to the camera.

Scroll your thumb along the side of the paper like the Teleprompter arrow. This will enable you to look up from the copy, deliver as much of the line as you can into the lens, and know exactly where you are when your eyes return to the page.

When performing an audition scene for a film or TV show you will usually get the script at least a day ahead. By the time you actually walk into the audition, you will have run the lines so many times that you will probably have them memorized. The temptation is to do it without a script since you know the words so well.

As a general rule, I would recommend keeping the script in your hand for the audition. You don't have to look at it. That's not why you've got it (but if you get a little nervous and "go up," it can come in pretty handy).

Actually, why you've got it is for psychological purposes — not yours, but *theirs*. Maybe the performance you're giving in the audition room is the absolute best acting you can do, but there's no reason to let the casting people know that. Since this is an audition, they don't expect to see your very best. They are sure that when you've had more of a chance to get familiar with the script, your final on-air performance will be better.

You want to keep them thinking that. If you do your audition scene without a script, it won't impress them that you've learned the words (anybody can do that), but it may make them think that they might be looking at the very best you can do. If you are holding a script, whether you look at it or not, it is still, clearly, an audition scene and you are automatically given the benefit of the doubt that your actual performance will be even better than your audition.

I think it's interesting how the odds can be thrown so much in your favor just by holding a script. Of course, this does *not* apply to tests. By the time you reach the screen test, you've already passed this point. The test is the time for you to pull out all the stops and be your most professional, most creative, most wonderful self.

As a professional film actor, especially in the beginning, you will find yourself auditioning much more than filming. This drives some actors crazy. I was fortunate enough to have been taught a trick many years ago which has kept me sane through many years of auditions.

It's just a little mental shift that makes all the difference. Nobody gets into this business because they want to audition; we get into it because we want to *perform*. The simple trick is to view each audition as a performance. Treat the casting people as your audience and be grateful to them for the chance they've given you to perform for them.

The only difference between an actual performance and an audition is the surroundings (and the pay check). As far as your mental and emotional approach to the work, there should be no difference.

This accomplishes a number of things. By facing it as a performance, your work will be better and stronger than if you thought of it only as an audition. You will have a good, professional relationship with the casting people, and you will get the satisfaction and fulfillment of a performance — the kinds of feelings that led us into this business in the first place.

CHAPTER SIXTEEN — SUMMARY

To audition on camera successfully, first of all, you need to learn as much as you can about what the casting director is looking for. You then want to *be* that person as much as you can as you walk in the door.

View your audition as a performance, and don't resent it — it shows.

Remember, whether you are working with cue cards or not, you want your audition to be as close to a polished performance as you can make it.

BOOK
TWO

INTRODUCTION TO BOOK TWO

The first part of this book was dedicated to the realities of acting on film. You now know who all those people hanging around the set are, what they're doing and why. You see how it all fits together. You also know what's expected of you as an actor and have received a few tips on how to live up to them.

We even looked at film acting, auditioning and how to better your chances of landing the job. Pretty comprehensive.

Actually, about the only part of an actor's life that we didn't touch on was… the actor's life.

Show business as a career carries with it unique mental, emotional, and psychological aspects. It's unlike any occupation in the world, and just like the awarenesses shared in the first half, few (if any) books are written about how to deal with it. There are certainly no classes on how best to handle life as an actor. Well, that's what we're going to deal with now.

What is it really like being a professional actor, and how does one go about avoiding becoming one of the many unfortunate statistics?

To make acting your profession (and to be successful and happy in the process) does require a certain mindset. The landscape here is different than in any other profession. There are no rules. You can work diligently for years and still have no guarantee of a pay-off.

On the other hand, the next phone call could change your life. How does one deal with the possibilities of such enormous "highs" and such devastating "lows"?

That's what we're going to deal with now. We'll discuss what some of the pitfalls are and how to avoid them. And how to set up your career in such a way that will maximize your chances of success while helping to insure that you will enjoy your life along the way.

It's an interesting road, traveled by relatively few, but one of the most unique journeys you can take.

Please enjoy.

CHAPTER 17

PROFESSIONAL POV

By the very nature of our business, actors come in all shapes, types and sizes. This is good. This provides the rich spectrum of characters that inhabit our TV shows and films. No effort will be made to ever try to find "sameness" here because this diversity is exactly what's required.

If a common denominator were to be found in all working actors, it would be in their attitude... their Point of View (POV) of the business and in their professional demeanor.

Let's consider that.

You'll notice that I put a lot of stock in "Attitude." I feel that it will not only determine how successful you will be, but also how much you will enjoy your life. Pretty important stuff.

Under the heading of "Professional Attitude" I would list such attributes as: reliability; professionalism (someone who knows what he or she is doing); and the ability to work with others (someone who realizes that filming anything is a team effort). (If you hadn't realized how much it was before, the first part of this book should have brought that to life for you.)

A seasoned professional uses his experience to anticipate problems before they occur and help others on the set who may not be as comfortable as they.

A professional is one who can be counted on. The producers and director feel the script is in good hands with this person. Other actors know they will always get the pro's best performance. We all know that good performances have the ability to raise the level of other performances around them. We like working with good actors.

To professionals, acting is a business; *their* business, an important business, and worthy of respect. It's also a very unique, different type of business, one which few people in the world know how to navigate.

A new professional watches and learns. If there happens to be a seasoned pro around, he will learn all he can from this person.

A seriously professional POV has such power that that, if handled badly, it can ruin lives. If handled well, it can bring rewards few occupations in the world can offer.

Now, that's not too intimidating, is it? Let's see what makes these superhuman professionals so great and what we have to know to become one of them.

STARVING ACTORS NEED NOT APPLY

Unless you're extremely well connected, nobody starts out at the top. Excellence in this business is achieved by working. The young actor still needs to study, learn and grow, but nothing replaces actually doing it.

Young actors try to get in any production they can for the experience. Most of these pay little or nothing. They generally have night jobs to keep day times open for interviews and auditions. Many of these jobs also pay little. The "starving actor" is almost a cliché. Times can get tough.

The point in bringing this up is — do not bring that Point of View with you. No one has ever been cast out of pity and they never will be.

Think about it. Shooting anything for TV and features is extremely expensive. It's also outrageously competitive. There are many choices available for every role. The casting director is going to bring in only the actors she thinks the producers and director are going to like. They, then, will give the role to the person they think will best handle it.

To all of them, the subtext of the "starving actor" is, "If you can't handle your own life, what makes you think you can handle this script?" You must face the script, the role, and these people with confidence. You've got to *know* that you are the best person for this role and convey that confidence to those doing the casting.

Of course, we also know that sometimes things really aren't going well. You might actually be broke and probably discouraged. It happens. *Do not let them see it!* Fake it! You're an actor — act! Act as though you are as confident as you wish you were (not cocky-confident, but solid).

As pertains to so much in this business, your attitude — your professional POV — can make all the difference. Sometimes it's as simple as how you look at things. You are not broke. You're just having a rocky spell that you haven't quite worked out yet but there is no doubt that you will. So until that happens, let's just get on with the creative moment at hand which may be to give a dynamite reading and audition and leave no doubt that they should hire you.

Actually, realize that that's exactly what they want you to do. They want you to be so good, so strong, that there is literally no doubt that this role should be yours. They don't want to worry about it.

There is also no reason for you to ever feel subservient or cowed by casting people. You are all equals. They need an actor they can count on for this role and, boy, are you ever that actor. Then show them.

Regardless of your finances, part of this confidence can come from your intimate knowledge of your product — you. There is an old acting adage that states, "The only thing you can bring to the role that no one else can, is you."

That's what you have to sell: *your* ability, *your* approach to the role, *your* mannerisms, look, vision, etc. You are the instrument you play. As such, it is your professional duty to take the best care of this instrument that you can.

THE TOP OF YOUR GAME

Eat well, sleep well, look your best, avoid excesses. Get and keep yourself strong and alert. If you want to play with the big guys, you've got to get to the top of your game and stay there. Give them the best you can be.

Sometimes this is hard to get excited about when you're waiting tables and behind on rent, but you never know when your break is going to come. One interview may lead to a film role, a series, soap, guest shot… maybe just a commercial but you might end up working with a director that may change the course of your life. (Remember, commercials are a good training ground for directors too.)

TIME MANAGEMENT

The way you manage your time is another area where you can impress people or aggravate them. This also may determine how much you enjoy each day. Actually, as an actor, you should already be very prompt. We learn the lesson of being on time very early. If the curtain is going up at 8:00, we *will* be in the wings, in makeup and wardrobe, ready to go on at 8:00 — period! There are no excuses. (Actually, our call would probably have been 6:30 or 7:00.)

Can you imagine a play not going on in time because an actor showed up late? "Gee, sorry. Traffic, you know?" That's an out-of-work actor talking.

Film is the same way. Directors generally try to start shooting at 8:00 a.m. The crew has been on the set or location since 6:00 a.m. setting up. Having a very expensive film crew hanging around waiting for an actor who hasn't shown up yet or is trying to hurry through make-up is not a good way to ensure job security.

Nor is it accepted well by anyone. The underlying message sent by those who are chronically late is, quite simply, that they don't consider you or the situation important enough to be on time. Traffic, appointments, phone calls, etc. really don't matter.

Basically, if the person really cared to be on time, they would have planned accordingly and been there — and they know it! They may not admit it (in fact, they won't) but they know it.

How you allot your time and what fits peaceably into your life differs greatly from person to person. Most of my adult life has been spent as a film actor and writer in Los Angeles. This is one career that you definitely have to have a certain temperament for. The life that I found enjoyable and stimulating would be horrible to many people.

First of all, you have to be a self-starter. You cannot sit around waiting for the phone to ring. That is death to an actor. If nothing's going on, you have to make something go on. This is also a business in which there is no security and every day is very different from the one before. There is no structure. The interviews are at different times, with me playing different parts for different people. (Sometimes there are two or three changes of clothes in my car.)

It seems there are always too many balls in the air: interviews, jobs, traveling, deadlines, other professional commitments and then, of course, there's real life and family. We have to get our cars fixed, too, and go shopping and take the kids to the doctor and school and soccer practice, etc. etc. All of which are important. Excuses do not apply.

195

As I mentioned, this is definitely not the life for everyone.

An actor friend of mine tells a story about Jack Nicholson years ago before he was "discovered." A group of actors were going to the beach one day and asked Jack if he'd like to go with them. He said he couldn't, it was during working hours.

"Working hours?" They didn't know what he was talking about. They knew he didn't have any interviews that day and he definitely wasn't shooting anything.

He explained that if he wanted acting to be his job he felt he should work at it as hard as anyone works at any other kind of job, namely, eight hours a day, five days a week. He dedicated himself to becoming a working professional actor and actually put in the hours to that end.

I imagine he had to get pretty creative to come up with things to do everyday but I'd say that work ethic has paid off for him in spades. He is now one of the highest paid and most successful actors in Hollywood. You might want to file that away. (Remember the old saying, "The harder I work, the luckier I get?")

PROFESSIONAL RELATIONSHIPS

Many have said of show business that it's "not what you can do, but who you know." While I don't agree with that totally, personal relationships can be extremely helpful. Just as beneficial, however, is building and maintaining good, professional relationships with the people already in your life.

I'm referring primarily to your agents (if you are in a market where agents are necessary) and the various casting directors you'll come in contact with. In larger markets, there will be many. Smaller markets may only have one or two.

In dealing with theatrical or commercial agents, it's necessary to walk a fine line. You don't want them to forget about you, you want to get and keep them interested and to think well of you, but you also don't want to become a pain.

I just reminded myself of an old acting joke: You know you're in trouble when you talk to your agent on Tuesday and he says "Have a nice weekend."

Sometimes it can happen. Let's see what we can do to not have it happen to you.

Be aware that most agents are quite busy looking after a list of actors like you that they represent. Actors who drop by unannounced just to say "hi" or keep them on the phone way too long are not appreciated. This is also true for casting directors.

The first step in dealing with these people is to respect them, their position, and their time. If you have an appointment, be prompt, be intelligent and friendly, but don't overstay your welcome.

If you feel it would be beneficial for your agent and you to get to know each other a bit better, ask him or her to lunch (you pay). You may have to book it a couple of weeks away but that's all right. That's the time to schmooze. (If there are a few agents in your agency, you may want to share a lunch with each of them. One every couple of weeks maybe.)

Let them know your strengths, history, goals, etc., but don't forget to ask about theirs, also. Many actors love to talk about themselves but unless they show some interest in the other person as well, their personal accolades may not mean quite so much.

(These meetings, incidentally, are not something that are done often. Once may be just fine.)

If you do happen to become friends over time, great, but still save it for lunch, weekends, or after business hours. They will thank you and respect you for it. (By the way, actors dating agents or casting directors is not a good idea if you wish to keep working. Keeping it professional is much better.)

Be aware of birthdays and holidays. A card is generally just fine, but if you really feel a gift is necessary, *think* about it. Have it not be too expensive (Don't try to "buy them" — they've seen that before.) but make it special. Something that shows you actually thought of *them*. No fruit baskets please. Be creative, memorable.

Remember, you are all equals. Not superior but definitely not inferior. You want to work. They make their money finding actors work. That's rather a nice fit. You need each other.

Be good at what you do, don't try to be the "personality kid," that gets very old. Above all, keep your problems to yourself and be the actor they can count on. That's the attitude that will get and keep you working over the years.

PRESENTATION

Besides your attitude, the face you show to the world determines how the world is going to view you. If you don't want to be thought of as a bum, I would suggest not looking or acting like one. If you wish to be thought of as a professional in this business, it's important to look and act the part.

We'll get more into this later but for now, let me just point out that every aspect of your professional life should be just that — professional.

> If you are going to an audition, dress and carry yourself according to the role.
> Be polite and respectful. Show how good and easy you would be to work with.

> Get the best pictures you can. Do not have your neighbor shoot them unless he's a damn good photographer. Your pictures represent you and are your first impressions to most people. This is not where you save money.
> Have your resume typed and laid out as cleanly and neatly as possible. If you don't have a lot of credits or aren't sure of the correct form, ask your agent. They usually have a format they like and will help you with it. If you don't have an agent yet, check out some other actors resumes. Borrow the format of the one that looks the most professional to you.

"Web Casting" is becoming more and more popular and is already the norm in some markets. Find out from your agents which are the main casting sites and get yourself listed on them. (It's not very expensive and is very important.) Sign up with as many as are considered professionally viable.

It really is important to get the best agent you can. All agencies don't get calls from all casting directors. The better the agency, the more and better calls you will get — as simple as that. Some agencies carry so much weight that just being with them makes you more respectable and desirable.

By the way, this also goes for managers. In some markets, having a manager as well as being with an agency is recommended. Managers have fewer clients than agents, therefore can put more personal attention on career building and getting you work. (That's the concept, anyway.)

If you can't get with one of these top agencies or managers at first, don't worry about it. Few can. Get the best ones you can, though, then move up when you start to get a body of work under your belt. There's not a stigma to changing unless you do it repeatedly. (But if an agent is getting you work, don't be in a hurry to leave even if a bigger agency is possible. An agent who believes in you and gets you worthwhile auditions is gold.)

Just know that everything you do — your attitude, your dress, your posture, pictures, resume, your promptness, how you answer the phone — everything goes toward your professional image. Know in your mind's eye how you want to be perceived, how you want to be thought of... then, one step at a time, start *being* that person.

AUDITIONING

Some actors get very upset at this business when they realize that there is considerably more time spent auditioning than actual filming ... sometimes 90% of your time in the early stages of your career. Months may go by without filming anything but if you and/or your agents are doing your jobs, there will still be auditions. Of course, they take time and pay nothing.

Still, you can't get the jobs without the auditions so the actors still go, hoping the next one will work out while trying to hide their resentment of the process.

I was an actor for 38 years and it seems I've spent half my life auditioning. Over time, I've seen many actors I'd been working and auditioning with get more and more bitter, griping and complaining. The fun had definitely gone out of the process for them.

That's a problem for actors. When the fun, interest, excitement and *joie de vivre* goes, so goes the twinkle in the eye, so goes your "specialness." It's hard to give an up-beat, spirited performance when your spirit feels flat. So... what do you do?

I had to answer that question myself. I like to live well and enjoy myself. Fortunately, I've been able to do that most of my life. I realize it's a privilege but I'm also prepared to work hard to bring it about. (But so are many people. Later, we'll discuss the difference between working hard and working *smart*.)

Years ago, while trying to make some sense out of my life (and "life in general"), I became aware of the saying, "It's not what happens… it's how you react to it." That made sense to me.

In my lifetime of "people watching" I've noticed that different people can have far different reactions to the same stimuli. An obstacle will crush one man while the same obstacle will make another man more determined.

A man loses a leg and spends the rest of his life with a cardboard sign by an off ramp. Another man loses his, gets a prosthetic, and runs a marathon. Their different quality of life was determined by their different reactions to the same misfortune.

(An interesting variation on this theme that I've always liked is, "You are not known by the names you are called, but by the names you respond to.")

When it came to a life filled with auditioning, I knew I had to come up with some sort of personal philosophy toward them, a positive POV, or I was destined to become one of those bitter actors myself.

I did. The wonder of philosophies is that they are generally just a matter of looking at the situation differently.

The first and most obvious one that came to me was to view it all as practice. When months go by without shooting something, you can get pretty rusty, which means you're not at the top of your game, which means your work isn't as good as it should be, which means you may never work again. Viewing auditions as practice for my acting proved very valuable.

Another point that occurred to me was that even if I didn't get this particular job, at least I was still "at the table." (As in poker, "You can't win if you're not at the table.") I was meeting industry people and actors on a professional level in a professional setting, which kept them all aware of me — an important thing to maintain as an actor.

But the very best POV, the one that made the largest difference, that kept me involved and made my auditioning the best it could be, was the simple observation that... there are no auditions. Only performances. View each audition as a performance. The casting director, director, producers, whoever's in the room, have invited you to perform for them. (Actually, that's what an audition is, isn't it? A mini-performance?)

Face it that way. Prepare your audition scenes with that in mind. While auditioning try to keep it as close to a "performing level" as you can. Be gracious to your audience and grateful for the opportunity to perform for them that day. (You don't actually say that, of course, your manner and attitude "convey" it. A simple "thank you" will be sufficient.)

This also makes it easier to not commiserate so much over the audition afterwards. ("How'd I do?" "Did they like it?" "Will they call?" "WHEN will they call?") Shoot your best shot during the audition and forget about it on the way to the car. If they want you, they know how to reach you. Time now to get on with whatever's next.

There you are, and it's really not too simplistic. It's just how we choose to react to the situation. This philosophy worked very well for me for many years. Hopefully it will for you, too.

BEING CENTERED

People wonder how an actor can stay centered and maintain personal sanity in a business that is so uncertain. I admit, sometimes that's a tough one. The first thing to realize is that that's the way the business is. Know that up front. There should be no surprises about this. This business is unique. The people who try to treat this business like any other are people destined for a very frustrating time.

Treat it like a business, yes, but it's not like marketing or accounting. Your MBA is going to do little here. You can borrow certain practices and a work ethic from mainstream business but then adapt them to the very distinctive aspects of show business.

One of the biggest problems unique to show business is the fact that so much of an actor's destiny is determined by other people. That is the nature of this business. Every job you get is because you were chosen over the other actors also considered for this role. (Even if you're a huge star, you're competing with other huge stars.) Every time you lose an audition, it's because they chose someone else.

Having your success determined by the whims of "they" is a pretty rocky foundation upon which to try to build a worthwhile life. But that's what we have to do. The trick is to set that life up so that you have as much control over it as possible. That's why I suggest you keep everything as simple and unencumbered as possible. Get the big house and fancy car when you can afford it, not when you may be able to borrow the money. There's a difference.

It's hard not to go crazy over each audition when you've got an hellatious mortgage and a hungry baby at home. If that is the situation, sanity will probably dictate that you have another job to rely on until you can get your show business to the point where you can count on it.

But realize, please, that even then, it will never be static. You may be hot for a few months, or years, things may slow up for a while, then you might get your series… or not.

In my 38 years of doing this, I remember counting when I was very hot that I was landing about one job in every five interviews. At my slowest, it was more like one in 50.

Do not delude yourself. If you know what you're facing and what the situation truly is, you can deal with it. Anything less is just confusing.

It may be wise to have another job at the beginning or, at least, another source of income, if possible. Having a certain amount of security can take the pressure off each individual interview. After a time, you will start to see a rhythm emerge.

Watch realistically your pace in the business. How many interviews are you going to? How many are you getting? Are you making enough from these to pay the bills? All of them? Are you pleased or at least momentarily satisfied with your agents? Are you getting to know casting directors (and they, you) or do you still feel like the new kid trying to meet everyone?

Do you find yourself going back to the same casting directors for various calls? (If you are, great. That shows that they are either requesting you or are happy enough with your work that they are accepting you when your agent mentions you. Professional relationships like this is what careers are based on.)

When you are working and interviewing so much as an actor that your other job is starting to get upset, and when your bills are or can be paid by your show business earnings, and when you are getting repeat calls from different casting directors, and the rhythm of it all makes you feel it's going to continue in this direction — that is the time to take the plunge and go full time.

A set-up like this should ground you sufficiently to do well and not drive yourself crazy.

Realize that film is just the canvas upon which you are painting; life is your subject. The more you know, the more you experience, the more you delve into the mysteries of most anything, the more interesting a person you will become and that makes for a more interesting actor. And that is definitely a "professional point of view."

CHAPTER 18

ARE YOU READY?

While a solid professional attitude is a must to make the most of your professional acting career, a thorough understanding of what this business entails is also mandatory. Before you throw yourself body and soul into the fray, let's make sure you're prepared for the battles ahead. We want as few surprises as possible.

There is so much printed about show business, it's hard to know the reality, especially looking from the outside in. One can get a pretty unrealistic view of the industry by reading the fan magazines.

It's important to understand the business as it *is*, not how you would like it to be. Stars in our eyes and big dreams aren't going to do us any good if they're not founded in reality. We don't want to just dream it, we want it to happen!

First of all, you must be aware of who has an actual chance of making it in this business. And that would be… everyone. Granted, there are more roles for some types than others, but since the range of TV and film extends so far, there are opportunities for success, even stardom, in all types.

You don't have to look like Brad Pitt or Julia Roberts to be a star (of course, if you do, it can't hurt). Who would have thought of John Candy or Chris Farley as star material? With her talent and attitude, Barbara Streisand went from the industry's ugly duckling to gracing the cover of *Playboy* magazine. Kathy Bates and Roseanne Barr are a couple others that show all sizes and shapes can make it.

One of the reasons it's important to face the business as realistically as possible is because you're going to have to sell yourself in it… and marketing Halle Berry is going to be quite different than marketing Whoopie Goldberg.

TYPE

Realistically, how do others see you? In no other business is it more important to know the answer to that question. You don't want people to have a certain sense of you, then have you walk into the audition as someone they're not expecting. Have your pictures and resume reflect the "you" that others see. That's the "you" you're selling. That's the "you" that's going to be seen on the screen.

By the way, you're not stuck with this image. If you want to change yourself, your stereotype, the type of roles you want to play, that's great, but it's important to know where you're starting from. What's the raw material you're working with? That's the "you" you are now.

If you are a fat person, it doesn't matter whether you like it or not, or that you're on a major diet. As long as you are a fat person, that's what you have to deal with and if you are going to be cast, you'll be cast as a fat person. Don't fight it. Be the best fat person in the world.

If you lose 50 pounds and change your image, change your pictures and attitude to reflect this "new you." (It would also be good to pay social calls to all the casting people so they can see this new person you've become.)

What's important is dealing with the reality of the situation — now! Your reputation will be built on the reality of "you," so don't you be the only one not aware of that reality.

By the way, this example is just that, an example. We all have imperfections we have to deal with. Maybe our nose is too big or our skin's bad or we're sure we're too tall, too short, too thin, etc.... but we need to deal with it. Remember, the scope of show business is as diverse as the many types of individuals in the world. There is, literally, no limit to what you can do or how high you can go… flaws and all.

AGE

Age is another factor to be honestly dealt with. As with "type," all ages work, but some work more than others. Most roles are for teens through the thirties. After that, most roles become more character in nature and fewer and farther between. If you can establish yourself somewhere while you are in that younger age range, it would be the best and easiest. If you can't, don't worry about it. Forge on.

Remember, this is also a generality. One of the narcotics of this business is that there are always going to be exceptions. The career you build will be yours alone. I can promise you, it will be like no one else's. What you do and how you do it is entirely up to you. While nothing is guaranteed, nothing is also out of the question.

One of the things I've always found interesting is that each year there are actors, especially in new TV series, that are really good, many in their forties and fifties… and I've never seen them before.

Where'd they come from? As I said, they're really very good. You usually only get to become that good by working, having some experience under your belt.

Probably, most of them have been working in theater, which may be the best place to hone your acting skills. Rehearsing for a month or two instead of a few hours in film and doing the same show for weeks or months really allows the actor to get into the character's skin. Because of time, filming usually doesn't allow that courtesy.

So here are these middle-aged actors appearing on the film scene in full glory. Perhaps they enjoyed theater better (as many actors do) but got lured to film by the money (which is much better). Perhaps they were too immature when they were younger or they might have been strapped by early responsibilities so that the first time they had to really give it all a go was when they were in their forties? Lot's of possibilities.

You should know that starting out in this business usually gets tougher as you get older but, obviously, it can still happen. Know the odds, know the likelihood, don't fool yourself, then get to work. Know also that there's no limit to what you can do.

Even though this business is different from any other, actors are still just people. There are no superhuman qualities necessary. The main difference is, like dancers or athletes, our product is ourselves and what we can do with it.

Introspection and self-study is perhaps more prevalent, and necessary, in our business than others but that's basically because we're in the business of pretending to be other people. (An actor friend of mine does a lot of cartoon voices. When people ask him what he does for a living, he says, "I pretend I'm other people and animals.")

As with "Type" earlier, in order to know where we're going and how to get there, we have to know where we're coming from. What does our basic canvas look like? That's us.

It's what we do with this product (us) and how we market it that determines our fate. I believe I mentioned before about being a "self-starter." That, perhaps more than anything, is the foundation for a career in show business.

There are no rules. No time cards. No protocol. No order. You and your specific circumstances determine what each day is going to be and each day is going to be different from anyone else's. Make these days count.

In the preparation process, be prepared to be creative. Meet people, create good relationships around you, not only with friends and peers but with your agent, manager, and casting directors. Learn and practice your craft. Keep yourself healthy and looking your best (for your type).

Put "you" in charge of your life as much as possible. Very important aspects of our lives are going to be determined by other people. All the more reason to get control over what we can.

We still determine how we live. By how hard and smart we want to work (i.e. other jobs and careful investing), we also decide our income level. By our education (self-taught and/or otherwise) we determine how smart we're going to be and what kind of a person we will become.

We're back again to how we react to a situation being more important than the situation itself.

SELF-IMAGE
The way the business and the world sees us depends very much on the face we show the business and the world… and that is based on our self-image. How we dress, how we walk into a room, how we meet people, what we realistically think our destiny is… in all this our self-image shows through,

What is your self-image like? The answer to that question may depend on how old you are, If you're a teenager or in your twenties, just starting out in life and this business, your self-image has probably not fully formed yet. One moment you may feel like you can do anything you want to and could conquer the world… but then there are times when you feel hopelessly deflated, like you can't do anything right.

As you grow older, these extremes lessen a bit although some vestiges of both will remain. Your self-image is another very important area in your life that you have complete control over. You shape your self-image.

Let's consider that. Regardless of age, take a good look at you as you are right now, physically, mentally, emotionally, even spiritually. Look for things that make you a little different from other people; a husky voice maybe? A scar? Do you have really good or bad hair? The ability to speak French? Maybe you're a really good fly fisherman? Are you calm, centered, flighty?

What do you like about yourself (not what you think others like, *you*)? Are you strong, solid, reliable, off-the-wall, creative, silly, fun, serious, intelligent, whacko? All these attributes are gold!

In the building of your professional self-image, some things may have to be changed or readdressed, but do not touch anything on those lists!

Go strictly after the things you don't like about yourself and/or things that don't fit into the image you want to show to the world and how you want to be thought of.

Would the person you want to be chew her nails? Go to interviews with dirty hair? Would they feel self-conscious or inferior going into an audition?

As you look into this, I think you'll find that 90% of this self-image is going to be attitude. It's very important that you like yourself (not "love," like is just fine). You've got to be proud of this product you're selling. You've got to feel that you deserve all these good things you're going after.

We'll get more into this in the chapter on "Competing," but realize that the feeling of being "less than" shows forth more obviously than any other. This will halt any chance of success before you even get started.

DRESS & GROOMING

As an actor, it's important that the image you have of yourself is the image you show the world. Realize that how you dress and carry yourself not only creates people's first impression of you but how you will be thought of afterwards as well.

The expression "you can't judge a book by its cover" is much more true with books than with people. You can tell a lot about people by the outer package they choose.

If you are going to dress in black, have tattoos up both arms and a ring through your nose, people are going to think of you in a certain way. You will probably be considered a bit hostile. You are probably not going to be considered for management. Parents will probably not be overjoyed by your dating their daughter (or son) — but you knew that before, didn't you?

Most everything people do in life is to find approval of some sort. People dress like the above to find favor with the group that's important to them and to let the rest of the world know that they couldn't care less about them.

From the vantage point of show business, this greatly limits the types of roles you'll be considered for… but like Vin Diesel or the Rock, careers can even be made out of that type.

This, of course, is an extreme example. (So is a three-piece grey flannel suit.) Just know that this is another area you have control over. You control your image and the way you will be perceived.

Consider who you are, who you want to be, and make your image a combination of them both.

A good place to research images is at the mall. Sit back and watch people go by, but categorize them as they go. What do the various dress choices and the way people act and carry themselves tell you about them? Are they nice, angry, lost, confused, on top of it, happy, not happy, secure, blue-collar, white-collar, dressed for success, dressed for failure, needy, or are they so nondescript that they don't say anything at all… as if the person inside didn't even have a personality?

Notice how you can answer the above questions with a glance. A first impression. It might be wrong but if it is, the person is giving an incorrect image to the world that they might not even be aware of. As an actor, you don't want to do that.

Think of the possibilities. Not only for character building but for yourself. Are there attributes or little things perhaps that you could adopt that could help your image? What was it about the people that made you think "Now, there's a good one"? Their clothes, their carriage, the attitude they emitted… a ready smile?

Try to figure it out and see if you could borrow a couple of things or adapt them for yourself? Look for role models.

Do not become a "fashion victim." Be aware of current trends, keep yourself up to date, but do not be dictated to by fashion. Deal with what works best for you and your image.

As you "people watch" be aware also of what doesn't work. Let their mistakes work for you so you don't have to make them yourself.

Know your assets. If you've got a great body, certainly take advantage of it… but do it in a classy manner. Understate it. Let your good points be discovered, not flaunted.

Also know that certain types of clothing look better on certain body types. You should be very aware of your body type; round, pear-shaped, long and lean, etc. This, incidentally, is something you're just going to have to deal with. You can't change your body type — but you can work within its confines.

A perfect example of this was one of the actresses I worked with on *General Hospital*. She shall remain nameless (because she'd kill me) but she was a major part of the cast for years.

Like most men (and women) I notice women's figures. I'd always thought of her as a well-built, attractive woman. She generally had her makeup done in her dressing room, so the only times I would see her was when she was on stage, at an event, or preparing to go home at the end of the day.

One morning she came in to the regular makeup room in her bathrobe while I was there. I couldn't believe what I saw. She was extremely pear-shaped and I mean extremely! I'd never noticed it before. It was like she'd gained 50 pounds overnight.

Later, when I saw her on the set, it was gone. She knew what styles worked on her and dressed accordingly. This awareness made her able to present to the world an image of herself that *she* wanted.

Get and keep that awareness about yourself. Have the way you dress accent the good aspects of your body while minimizing the points you don't like. There are many books dealing with various body types, and many sales people are quite knowledgeable about this sort of thing. Don't be afraid to ask them. Explain (or show them) the situation and see what they would suggest for you. Give it a shot.

GETTING CLOSER
We've been laying the background for your new acting career or your

existing one that could use a face-lift. We've worked around the periphery but have neglected the core. Bottom line — you've got to be a good actor. You have to know your craft.

As stated, this is not an acting book. There are many that are quite good and many capable teachers. All I can do here is to urge you to get at the top of your game and stay there. Books alone won't do that. You must work with other actors.

How you go about that is up to you. You can take scene study classes where you have to (or get to) perform every week. Or, if you have a good group of actor friends, do scenes with them. An enjoyable way to work on your sight-reading is to have a "play reading." Get a handful of actors, put chairs around in a circle, everybody take a couple of parts and do the whole play. It's a good, fun way to keep your chops up.

In this business, one phone call could change your life. That's the good and bad news. If you are not prepared when that call comes though, haven't acted in a while, maybe, or gained a few pounds that you haven't gotten around to losing… you may blow that opportunity.

There may be other chances just as good, there may not be. You don't know. What we do know is that if you take advantage of a break when it comes, one may be all you'll need.

The next tip is something that I've done all my life. I was surprised to learn that many people don't — so, I'm mentioning it here because I feel it's beneficial. What it is, simply, is to plan out meetings and business phone calls in advance. Run the two- or three-sided conversation in your head as you would like it to go and as you think it may go. (Sometimes in the car on the way to the meeting is a good time.)

Keep in mind always where you want the conversation to go. What do you want out of it? What is the goal, the purpose of the meeting? Focus.

Come up also with worse-case scenarios. How would you react if it happened? What are some questions they may ask? Be sure to have good answers, practice them. (Saying them aloud makes them more specific than if you just think them.) You don't want to be stuck for an answer.

Make sure the questions you want to ask are thought out and intelligent ones. Anticipate problems that might arise. For example, you might not have a lot of experience. Why do you still feel you could handle this role? Have an answer for them. Think it out, put the experience you do have in the very best light. Practice it.

After you've done this in your head a bit, be critical. Does it need something? Is it a little bland, maybe? Then spice it up. Conjure up an anecdote, maybe something related that was rather silly. Don't strain or push. Everything still has to come out naturally.

What you're doing is preparing guidelines, not a script. You plan ahead, then prepare to improvise — just like acting.

Here's another little preparation tip to add to your people watching. We discussed the mall in regards to dress but take it beyond that to watching real people acting like real people. Reality shows are no good for this, they still know they're being photographed. You want absolutely real actions and reactions.

How do people really greet each other, treat their kids, talk with a salesman, act when surprised? Does someone talk with their hands in an interesting way? Could that be used in a character?

Do people look each other in the eyes when they talk? If not, where do they look? What does that convey? Try to pick out little, subtle nuances that might make a character more interesting.

215

Watch your own reactions. Actors are notorious for filing away emotions at the most inopportune times. You may be breaking up with your boyfriend and notice you've gone through half a box of Ritz crackers in the last half hour. Hmmmm.

When a close relative died, you noticed that your first reaction was to smile. What? You loved that person. Why did you do that? Disbelief maybe? Someone joking? Interesting. Perhaps you can use that someday.

Weddings are another place where many people don't act like one would imagine… and funerals… or parties. Before you know it, you'll become an expert at the fine art of "people watching" … and your acting will be all the better for it.

CHAPTER 19

COMPETING

Competition and competing successfully are constants in a show business career. From the lowliest industrial film to the biggest blockbuster movie, if you are cast it's because you beat out the other actors vying for the part. If you didn't, they beat you.

Healthy competition is something you're going to have to face and get good at if you are to have a full-blown career. I should probably underline that first word; *healthy* competition.

This is ability against ability. There's no hate here. Remember our discussion about people working with people they think they could work well with? Think for a moment how "hate" shows. You don't want to bring that into the audition room with you. It is destined to do you no good.

This is professional competition like you find in professional sports. Very seldom do the players actually hate each other. Actually, off the court or field, they're probably close friends, but when they're pitted against each other they each do their best to win the contest. Then they go home and forget about it and live to fight another day. So it is with acting.

BRING YOUR BEST

Also like professional sports, it's necessary to give your very best if you want to win and keep winning. Slackards get found out quickly. If you find yourself belittling a script you don't care for or "walking through" your interviews, you'll also find that you're losing jobs to those who are taking it all a bit more seriously.

Besides, having you and your peers all bringing their best is a win-win. If you're auditioning against a certain person a lot and they seem to be booking everything, what are you going to do? You could quit and find another occupation, or you could find out what they're doing better than you and set about bettering yourself in that area until you start winning your head-to-head battles.

A perfect example is the arrival of Tiger Woods on the golf scene. He beat everyone the first few years because he was, quite frankly, better than everyone.

But the other pros were just that — pros, and they got busy. They got better. They had to. Tiger is still among the frontrunners but now he has company. His bringing his best to the game ended up making everyone better.

I had a situation like that a few years ago. A buddy of mine (my tennis doubles partner, actually) was the same general type as I am so we found ourselves competing for the same roles a lot. For about a year, it seemed like he got everything. It was very frustrating.

I worked on my delivery, my attitude and my "look" over and over. If something didn't work, I tried something else. Finally, I turned it around and *I* started booking. I got better and he chased me for a while. I liked that part.

That started a great time for me. I was working pretty much nonstop for a couple of years or so. I was all over the television. I remember going to a certain interview one day, had just finished reading and was on my way out when a young actor I didn't know, who was also up for the part, called out after me in the nastiest voice he could summons, "What do you want!" He yelled. "To do everything? Don't you ever get enough?"

I was amazed. I left the audition saying nothing to that unhappy young actor but it affected me enough that I thought about it. Was I doing something wrong? Was I being selfish? Should I be thinking more about the "greater good"?

What I came up with was "no." I had only to think back a couple of years when I couldn't get arrested. Remember, I had a family and house payments to worry about also. I wasn't just doing this for the fun of it.

When everything is going your way, enjoy it. Shoot what you can. Just generally try to take advantage of the situation as much as you can because you never know how long it's going to last.

But please, don't hate the actors that are having the success you wish you were. In time, maybe a short time, that could be you. Learn what you can from others during the lean times. That will bring on the good times that much sooner.

Be sure to realize that "working better" for an actor may be to work "easier." Maybe you're working too hard right now. Take a look. If an actor's job is done right, it looks effortless. No one wants to "see the work." It should appear natural and easy.

Actually, you should feel nothing but respect for your fellow actors. As you're finding out, being a professional actor is a difficult road. They're going through what you are. Competing and working together over the years will drive you all to a higher level of expertise.

Besides, you will become good friends with some of these actors. Few people in the world understand what you deal with on a daily basis. These are your peers. You know and can appreciate each other like no one else.

219

In many interviews you'll find yourself playing a scene with another actor. Even though you may have your competitive juices stirred up, *do not compete with this actor!* The point of having you read with another actor is to see how you work with others in general and with this actor specifically. You're being looked at *together*.

Trying to out-do your scene partner could very effectively knock both of you out of the running. You will definitely not be showing the casting people what they are looking for.

Your scene partner may be a bit upset with you, too, if you go down and drag him with you. Conversely, the more you work together and help each other (by listening, reacting fully and honestly, not hogging camera angles, etc.), the better off you both will be.

Regardless of whether or not either of you gets the job, giving a full professional read with this other actor will leave him respecting you and that's the beginning of a professional relationship — a very good thing to have. (And the fact that his father may be the next Steven Spielberg doesn't hurt any either.) What goes around, comes around.

Just a couple more quick points about auditioning. Through my years in the business, I've found myself on the other side of the casting table a few times. What I discovered there surprised me.

I felt I knew seconds after an actor walked into the room whether they were right or not. Sometimes before they had even said anything. I was ashamed.

I felt it was bad of me, jumping to judgment and not giving each actor his due, until I mentioned this to other casting people who did this for a living. They said it happens all the time, in fact, it is the norm. Occasionally an actor can change the initial opinion that was formed by doing a stand-out audition but very rarely. Nine out of ten times the first impression sticks.

What we can learn from this is… go into the audition room *as the character*. You've got roughly nine seconds to land that first impression. Be aware of that. (This, incidentally, could be the single most important observation in competitive auditioning.)

That piece of info made a big difference in my auditioning. Perhaps you feel like I did, that it would be more interesting and impressive for the casting folks to see what a good actor I was by walking in the door as one person and becoming another in front of them. Sounds like a good plan, doesn't it?

Wrong. The person walking through the door is the one they remember. This may be different for theater, where time is not so much of an issue. There is plenty of time before "curtain" to get into your role. In film, shooting out of sequence, on and off all day, everyday, producers and directors are just more comfortable with someone who is the role.

The way they look at it is that they won't have to wait around while you become this college professor or this hardened military type. They'll just hire someone like that. They only want to see the role. That's you, coming in the door as the character.

Prepare in the waiting room, take a big breath before walking into the audition room, become the character, then walk through the doorway and nail it.

LEARNING

Learning from others can take many forms. One of the best and cheapest ways is to become a critical audience when watching a film or TV. First of all, see who's working in your age range and general type. Who's booking the roles you'd be good for? Try to discover as much as you can about what they've got going for themselves. A unique look? An individual approach to the material? An acting style of their own?

Or did they just get there first? Maybe all they've got that you don't have is a fatter resume and momentum. That's important to know, too.

So, what do you have to do to compete with that person? Pop your performing skills up a notch? Maybe get a better agent or light a fire under yours so that you can get the interviews that would allow you to go head to head with these people? Get feedback from agents, managers, casting folks, actors you know and respect... anyone. Analyze the situation, come up with a plan or two and get after them.

The very best person to learn from in the audition room or while shooting the project, is the director. Listen very closely to him. (Remember, it's the director's vision of the script that gets filmed.) The director wants you to be excellent, to be the absolute best you can be, and he'll tell you how to do it. Try to understand as much as you can, exactly what he wants from you and your performance.

You'll grow as an actor and do the job well at the same time. Let there be no competition between you and the director at any time. You should always be very much on the same page. (If there is a problem, remember, the director is your boss. If there's any changing to do, you'll be doing it.)

If the project comes out well, you will both be given accolades. If not, you will share the blame. Your fates are intertwined.

Please don't feel that learning from others will, in any way, make you any less unique. First of all, you adopt only what you consider to be people's *good* traits, and then you *adapt* them to your own personal style. You don't act like they do (*they're* already doing that). You make these certain traits your own.

If you love someone's sense of humor, for example, you don't mimic their sense of humor but you may want to bring yours out more... maybe have a little more fun with everything.

If you see a certain look on someone that is very effective, you don't go out and buy that identical outfit but you might want to try on something in the same style. See if it works for you. Adapt.

This is an ongoing process, incidentally. It's good to take an objective look at yourself every now and then to see how you're doing. Are you still conveying the image of yourself that you want to? Has your self-image changed over the last weeks, months, years? Has your outward presentation of yourself changed with it? Should it?

Don't let yourself get too predictable or boring. Keep trying things. Keep learning. Keep growing.

THE WHOLE PACKAGE

Realize that everything about you comes into play in these competitions. It all comes down to how you make people feel about you in regards to the role being cast. What kind of shape you're in physically is a big part of that. So is your mental acumen. How sharp are you? Do you emit an aura of confidence?

And, of course, your ability. That's always in there. You still have to deliver the goods. If you're not comfortable with your personal level on any of the above, you might have some work to do.

Remember, *you* are the product you are selling. Take the very best care possible of this product, keep it up to date, give it every chance you can to succeed.

In order to be thought of at all in this business, you have to bring something to the table. It's also important for you to know what it is. Casting people are going to wonder why they should cast you.

Know why. Not a slick, flip answer but *really*. Why should they hire you? What are your main attributes (really handsome, funny looking, great build, character look)?

If you're not sure, think what made you want to be in pictures in the first place? What made you think you could do it (talented, great voice, outgoing personality)?

I had an interesting situation when I first got started. I had been a musician by night (singing and playing guitar in clubs) but was a disk jockey by day. It was a small radio station where practically every commercial, as well as the news, was read by me.

Since I was also playing records and keeping the log, there was no time to look anything over. Everything was sight-read on the air, first time through.

The result was that by the time I first hit Hollywood, I was an excellent sight-reader. I could do a better job sight-reading a script than most actors could do after studying it for an hour.

What the producers didn't know was that that was pretty much what they were going to get out of me at the time. The other actors might have been better than me actually doing the part, but since everyone feels that after studying the script and being directed, one's performance will be much better than the audition, I got the benefit of them thinking my performance also would be much better. Alas, many times it wasn't. But it got me going.

It was off that ability that I got my first few roles that enabled me to start growing (and learning!) in the business.

Early on in my career, those roles led to me going under contract to Universal Studios. One of the fellows there with me was David Hartman. David did a lot of TV years ago and a few movies (one with me: *Nobody's Perfect*) and starred in his own TV series, *Lucas Tanner*, before moving to New York and hosting *Good Morning America* for 12 years. Not a bad career.

The way it started is what's interesting. When David first came to Los Angeles, the only film he had of himself was a 30-second commercial with him as a cowboy. That was all. But it did show his six-foot-six-inch frame and his long, toothy, friendly face. On the strength of that alone, he got his Universal contract. (Just in case you were thinking that you didn't have enough experience to land something good.)

David loved photography and he made it work for him in a way I'd never seen before. On every show he worked on, he made a point of not only meeting the "big guys" (producers, director, cinematographer) but also the "little guys" (grips, sound men, lighting, etc.).

During the course of a shoot, he would take candid shots of everyone doing their jobs: setting lights, holding boom mics, taking scripts notes, whatever. Toward the end of the shoot, he would hand out the pictures to everyone, mounted, personalized and autographed. The crew loved them.

It wasn't long before the word around the studio was that David Hartman was the greatest guy in the world. Obviously that's a pretty nice place to be. Soon, when opportunities and openings occurred, the powers-that-be started thinking about that tall, lanky guy they'd heard so much about.

David was up to the task, and was soon off and running. He used his hobby to separate him from the crowd. That's part of looking for your own uniqueness. Is there something in your life that you may be able to take advantage of like that?

We mentioned before the diversity of types in the film industry. It's important that you understand "you" very well to best identify your uniqueness. Where do you fit in to this spectrum? Are there others like you? *Lots* of them? How are you different? Is this difference apparent or are you going to have to make people aware of your difference?

The people running casting sessions sometimes see, literally, hundreds of people over a few days for many different parts. Can you imagine how exhausting and confusing that would be? Can you see how faces and performances would all start to run together after a while?

Try to identify your "uniqueness" and how to show it. Give your agents something to work with. Give the casting directors something to remember you by. What that would be depends upon your personality and the personality of your agent and the casting director. (Here's where a life lived interestingly can come in handy.)

Get creative. Send flowers, nuts, or candies for birthdays, or take them to lunch. If they have a collection of something, perhaps you could add to it. (If appropriate and not too expensive. If it is, at least it could be a topic of conversation.) Try to find out about special hobbies or interests (like woodworking or Pilates).

Sports are always good common denominators if you know they're interested or good at something. (But remember, quickly. Don't take up too much extraneous time at auditions chatting. A mention would be just fine. Maybe a question to show you're interested. That's all.)

Try to make your audition memorable. If there is an obvious way that the dialogue you're reading will probably be done by everyone, try to tweak it a little. Perhaps come at it from a slightly different angle, still keeping with the sense of the scene, of course. Make it your own. Individualize it. Don't think strictly how the scene *should* be played, think also how it *could* be played.

As we discussed in "Professional POV," an air of confidence should underlie everything you do in this business. Before anyone can be impressed by you to the point of hiring you, they have to feel that *you* know you can do it.

They want to hire the best. They have to feel confident that their script is going into capable hands. Your job is to make them feel that way about you. I can promise you, those competing against you are trying to do the same thing.

To compete well, it's necessary to know as much as you can about the role. Try to learn exactly what they are looking for, then give it to them. The actor that comes the closest gets the job — as simple as that.

What if you were given a call as an engineer? You went off to the audition in your best railroad suit only to find you were supposed to be an electrical engineer? Ask many questions.

I had a situation a number of years ago that underlines the importance of staying flexible. I had just finished shooting an episode of *Hawaii 5-0* where I played a priestly-type guru, preaching on the beach to my followers and running my little commune.

Not long after returning state-side, I got a call from the same casting director asking me if I'd like to play another guru for *General Hospital*?

I said, "Sure." Imagine my surprise when I got the script that this was a "Manson"-type guru. Totally different. So, I shifted gears and, as things in this business happen sometimes, good things come from unexpected directions.

The *GH* guru job was only for five or six shows and had me in long bushy hair and heavy beard. The powers-that-be liked what I did and asked me back a month or so later to play a new doctor on the show (looking like myself, this time). I stayed there for the next four years and had a wonderful time.

That story exemplifies a couple of points we've talked about.

227

1) Getting repeat calls from the same casting director. Doing a good job for them lets them build confidence in you and makes them want to submit you for other things.

2) This is a perfect example of one job being an audition for the next. I didn't even know about the upcoming doctor part, but I didn't need to.

With this in mind, no matter how bummed out you are, no matter what's happening in your life or how puny you may feel, never "walk through" a part. Always give it your all, shoot your best shot. You never know who's watching or what could happen.

CHAPTER 20

SUCCESS AND FAILURE

As a young actor, I realized full well how capricious and fickle this business can be. Even then, I'd seen a number of would-be actors dedicating their lives to this business but having little or no success. I didn't want to become one of them.

In my 25-year-old wisdom I made a vow to myself that if I hadn't "made it" by the time I was 35, I'd quit and go into another line of work.

The next ten years were interesting. I starred in movies, did guest-appearances on TV shows... and spent some time in the unemployment line.

When age 35 rolled around for me, I was divorced, alone, and out of work. It was not a good time. I felt like a total failure. But I also knew I wasn't through. There were irons in the fire, possibilities. I had a body of work behind me that hoped I could parlay into work ahead of me. Needless to say, I didn't quit.

Good thing. By the time I turned 40, I was married, had a son, and was a regular on the number one–rated show in America. Not bad. Show business can be like that.

The main lesson here, I imagine, is not to be too quick in labeling something a success or failure. Lives and careers are not black or white. Nor are they static. Everything is in a state of flux. Success and failure are transitory terms.

From my story above, we can also see that they are personal terms. I felt like a failure at 35, but to someone who had had no success at all, what I had already done could have labeled me a success in their eyes. It's all a matter of perspective, making it important that we each know what success means to us individually and have a plan to achieve it.

It has been said that "men never plan to be failures, they simply fail to plan to be successful."

Something as important as this deserves some looking into. That's what this chapter is about.

Because of the subjective nature of success, I would caution against over-defining it. As you change and grow, in knowledge and circumstance, your view of success will change, too. Good. That's the way it should be.

Too narrow a definition of success can stop you from enjoying life-changing possibilities. If the young Alex Trabec, who wanted to be an actor, had defined success for himself only as an actor, he might not have been interested when the *Jeopardy* job came around and would have missed out on a marvelous career.

Always be flexible. Success can come from where you least expect it.

FEAR OF FAILURE

No one wants failure in their lives and certainly no one wants their life defined by it. Failure, to most people, means an inability to achieve what they set after. Failure, then, is as subjective as your ideas of success.

Fear of failure at most anything has probably stopped more people from pursuing goals or taking actions than anything else. (If you're not sure you can do something, why put yourself up for possible ridicule by even attempting it?)

In show business, this fear seems even bigger. Our successes are up there on the stage or screen for all to see, but then, so are our failures... or is it the inability to get on that stage or screen in the first place that constitutes the failure?

What about all the little daily failures, the auditions that we didn't book (for the play, the commercial, the film)? Are these all failures?

In some circles just openly declaring that you want to be an actor or actress is cause for laughter. Everyone knows the odds are against it and may feel you are a fool for even trying. They just sit back and watch, waiting for you to fail... at least, it seems that way.

That's pretty scary stuff. One can certainly see how "fear of failure" could definitely enter in here.

But there's another emotion that must be dealt with also, that is just as strong as failure and just as debilitating. That is "I wonder if I could have?"

By never seriously putting yourself in the arena, you may never have given yourself an honest chance to succeed. Wondering if you "could have" can stop you from ever being totally fulfilled and effectively sap all the joy out of life. It must be addressed.

"Only those who dare to fail greatly can achieve greatly."

There is no failure in trying. The failure comes by not learning from the situation. Maybe show business won't work out for you. Okay, then you would know. You gave it a shot and can now get on with the rest of your life.

Is that failure? I don't think so. You've probably got a very interesting and unique chapter in your life that you'll always have, plus, you're free to live on without regret. Anything that brings that around is gold.

But what if you don't fail?

FEAR OF SUCCESS

A little less obvious is the "fear of success." At first glance, we wonder why success would cause fear. Aren't we all actively working toward that? Being a successful father, husband, businessperson, actor, golfer, everything?

On the surface, yes, but we also know success usually comes from going that extra mile. It's that extra effort that fear affects, especially in this business. Because of the extraordinary public interest in virtually all aspects of show business, big success and big failures are known worldwide. That kind of possible exposure is daunting.

It's also well chronicled how difficult it is for movie stars to stay married and stay sober, stay off drugs and maintain any semblance of a personal life. If you thought this is what success held in store for you, you might think twice about it, too, don't you think? (Consciously or subconciously.)

Well, the good news is that the above situations affect less than 1% of actors. We all are in the public eye somewhat but, believe it or not, you really do have some control whether to be a "fan magazine" target or not.

With success comes a certain amount of familiarity — you will get recognized by strangers every now and then and will sign the occasional autograph — but unless you end up in that 1% you will not be mauled every time you go out in public.

To try to find the facts of this matter, see what you can learn about the actors and the careers you respect (not necessarily the "fan mag" group). By following that lead, you'll find positive role models, people who are doing what you'd like to do and are making it work.

They're not quite as interesting for the "rags" to write about because they're more like regular folks, like you and me. It can and is being done.

One interesting aspect of fame that I never thought about until I experienced it is how vulnerable people make themselves to you. By placing you on a pedestal, they lower themselves beside you. They give you the power to hurt them very easily; a look, a sneer, a comment. They are open and susceptible.

But they can just as easily be affected positively. They give you so much power that you can bring much joy by hardly doing anything: a smile, an autograph, taking a minute to have your picture taken with them. It requires little or nothing on your part, it takes a few seconds, and you have a fan for life. That person will tune in your TV show, buy tickets to your movies, and tell everyone about the time they met you and what a fine person you are.

Plus, you made their day. Not a bad return for a couple of minutes, wouldn't you say?

Of course, you do have to keep your ego in check. By everyone making themselves lower than you, you might start thinking that you are actually "higher than they are." You're not. You're just in a different line of work.

It's helpful to have "just plain folks" around you to point out if you start believing your fan mail. It's tempting, especially at first, but it soon becomes just part of the game.

Let's take a look at some of the aspects of show business we're going to be dealing with, most of which are indigenous only to this profession.

One observation few people make in starting down this path, is that the acting profession, for most, is not a career for a lifetime. There are many more roles for actors in their twenties than in their thirties, fewer still for actors in their forties, fifties, etc.

So what happened to the actors who were working in their twenties but not in their forties? They moved on. They're doing something else now. They may still be a part of the business (teaching acting, being agents or managers, working for studios, etc.), they're just not primarily acting anymore. Many go on to something else entirely. Are these people failures?

Think of all the actors you've seen in your lifetime who have had hit series and been household names for years, only to disappear when their series ended. Or the movie star who seemed to be in everything for ten years or so, then nothing. What happened?

I'm afraid we're back to the capriciousness of the business again.

The joke in L.A. is that on the back of every actor's neck is a bar code that states; "Do not use after *such-and-such* a date." Of course, we don't know the date and it's different for every actor, but the industry seems to know. There's just a time when it's over.

Like being an athlete, a dancer, singer, newscaster, or talk show host, few have careers that last lifetimes. Styles change, what's hot, what's not.

Success also carries a responsibility that not everyone wants to accept. Once you've done exceptional, successful work, everyone expects your future work and career to be just as successful. People's expectations become high. Sometimes too high. Not all those successful actors who disappeared actually wanted to go, you know.

As Irving Berlin said, "The toughest thing about success is that you have to keep on being a success. Talent is only a starting point in this business."

I mentioned earlier that you couldn't duplicate someone else's career if you tried. Yours will be yours alone, no matter what happens. That's another reason to not be too quick to label something a success or failure.

At the beginning of your career, you may have very definite ideas about what constitutes success. Once you get immersed in it and start working professionally, those boundaries can change. The possibilities are endless.

There's much more to show business (and to show business careers) than movies, TV series, and Broadway. There are commercials, industrial films, announcing, off-Broadway, off-off Broadway, touring companies, broadcasting, game and talk shows, character voices and cartoons... and they are all show business.

Actually, they are all various forms of acting. Behind each of those categories are hundred of people and different classifications of behind-the-scenes jobs (directing, producing, writing, camera work, lighting, designing, etc.), and they're still show business, too. One is definitely not better than another. There are a lot of possible moves "sideways" in this business.

When I was first starting out, I remember a cute young girl who was studying with the same drama coach I was. She was quite good but wasn't having much luck working. After a year or so, she left. No one knew what happened to her.

A couple of years later, I was shooting a show in Phoenix. Part of it was shot in a TV station there, I was walking down the hall, when I heard "Hey, Steve!" I turned around to see the actress who had left. She looked great. It turned out that she was one of the main news anchor people at that station. She was extremely successful and loved it.

It would be a very narrow definition of failure if one were to put that label on her because her acting career hadn't worked out. She was on top of the world.

Perhaps a good definition we could work with would be "Personal success is simply the fulfillment of what makes you happiest."

Many actors start out dreaming about life in New York or Los Angeles but might end up in a summer stock company in Florida or a Shakespearean company in Ashland, Oregon — and love it!

Life can be much simpler and more manageable in small markets. The huge city is not for everyone and successful careers can be built most anywhere.

Success, failure and all points in-between are very much in the eye of the beholder. It depends upon your point of view whether you are thrilled or not. Knowing yourself is quite important in this.

As a young wannabe actor in Cheyenne, Wyoming, I knew I had to go to New York or Los Angeles to try to break into the "bigs." Thank goodness I turned right and went to L.A. first. What I found out about me later was that I would have been miserable in New York, even if I had been successful!

Success in New York terms usually includes long theatrical runs like having a show running for a couple of years on Broadway. Doing two years of eight shows a week of the same show (same character, same dialogue, etc.) would drive me nuts.

Film suits my personality better. Movies usually take a few months to shoot, TV shows — a week or so, even in a series, I might be playing the same character for a few years but in each episode I'm doing something different, always a new problem. I like that.

My wife is just the opposite. She was a professional dancer and had quite a varied career. Among her favorites was the three years she spent with *Evita*. She loved the steadiness of it, the security, working and perfecting moves over time, plus, she just loved the show. It suited her perfectly.

You don't want to find yourself in a place in your career where you are "successful" but unhappy. It can happen.

During my years on *General Hospital*, there was an actor I respected greatly named Peter Hanson. Peter is a great guy, in his sixties (then), grey, very handsome, a fine actor and had been on *GH* for many years.

I knew that he had done some major films when he was younger and asked him one day if he missed all that. Why had he stayed on a soap for so long? He just looked at me and smiled.

"Let's see," he began. "I have a lovely house, I fly my own airplane, my children have all gotten through college, I've been able to work practically daily at my craft and haven't been out of work for nearly 20 years."

I didn't have any more questions. He was a successful, happy man. I also realized something else: Successful people don't need to convince you how good or successful they are. They're not doing it for you.

REJECTION

The amount of rejection in show business is legendary. People on the outside wonder how we can take it. Doesn't it beat you down?

The answer to that is, "Yes, sometimes it does, but most of the time, it doesn't." I'll explain.

After someone has been in this business about a month, he learns what we discussed in "Competing," that we are always going to lose more auditions than we are going to win and we take the "personal" part out of it.

It wasn't that they didn't like *me* (they don't even know me). They didn't think I was right for the part. In that, they were either right or wrong. Perhaps they were right and I really wasn't right for the role. (It happens.)

But, if they were wrong and I actually would have been great for the part, I have some work to do. Perhaps they didn't know what I could do or they weren't aware of my range and ability. I'd have to work on correcting that.

The way professionals react to negativity is much more analytical and professional than just putting our tail between our legs and slumping home.

However, we are human. Dry spells can be particularly difficult. The longer they go on, the harder it is to keep ourselves "up" and positive. Occasionally there are also roles that stand out over the others. These are the ones we *really* want. It's also tough when we lose them. They don't come around that often.

The only thing we can do is to face it professionally and like a baseball pitcher who's in a slump, just keep throwing. His coach and your agent will both tell you the same thing, keep after it. It won't last forever. Hang in there, you just have to wait it out.

That's what we do because, basically, we have no alternative. Sometimes it can get tough, but remember the first part of this example. Most of the time we face it like a numbers game; the more interviews we go on, the more jobs we'll get. We shoot our best shot then forget it. They know how to reach us.

Actors, many times, don't have to look further than themselves to find someone to beat up on them. For example, an actor does a play that is reviewed by six writers. Five loved it. One thought the actor wasn't strong enough to carry the show.

That actor could be morose for weeks thinking that people believed he was too weak for the role. The five glowing reviews have been forgotten. The bad one, he can't get out of his head.

Actors can be like that. We have to watch it. Some actors who are severely handicapped by questionable reviews make a point of never reading them. Much better for their peace of mind as well as their subsequent performances.

We have to believe we have a reason to be in this business, that we have something to contribute. Auditioning is our opportunity to show what we can do. If we are unable to sufficiently convince others of our ability, we have to work on that. Rejection points out our weak points.

They are either so very weak that we end up in another business (or another facet of this one), or we get to work to make our weak points some of our strongest.

As Confucius said, "Choose a job you love and you will never work a day in your life."

Realizing that acting may not be the only occupation we'll have in our lives, it's important to be aware of a few things.

The first is to enjoy it while it's here. Remember those glowing reviews also, remember the good auditions, the good shows.

Don't dwell on the negative because, as we've just read, there's plenty to go around.

239

There's also a lot of enjoyment to go around. People pick this profession because they enjoy it. So please do, warts and all. You know sometimes it's going to be difficult.

Please don't view every setback as a failure. Don't be too hasty to categorize yourself. You haven't seen how it all plays out yet. A career in show business is a *process*. You're always in a state of going up or going down. As such, success or failure is a label to be used at the end of one's life looking back over it all.

I think you'll find that you failed at some things but succeeded at others. You decide if it was worth the trip.

CHAPTER 21

SHOW BUSINE$$

Perhaps you've noticed a recurring theme in this book is to be realistic. To see things as they *are*, not as we would wish they were or what we think they *should* be.

Nowhere is dealing with the facts of the matter more important than in the business end of things. Brutal honesty is what's going to keep us out of trouble. It'll keep the rent paid, our taxes up to date, and we might even be able to afford a meal or two.

Since show business is a business like no other, it requires planning for unique eventualities. The first consideration, and the primary need for planning is that there is no way to know up front exactly how long your career may be.

Realize that even if you have a long, healthy one, it won't be a straight line. There will be great months and years and not-so-great ones. Plan accordingly. What would you do if...?

Now, don't just deal with the negative here. Sure, you should know how you're going to live if things don't work out but also spend some time on how you'd deal with your fortune if you hit it big. How would you invest the money from your smash TV series?

Best- and worst-case scenarios should be looked at here, too. Best case: You'll go from your series into a string of major motion pictures. But realize also, that things could slow up a bit after your series goes off the air. Both possibilities should be considered.

(Remember those big stars we talked about who we haven't seen in years? Some are set up for the rest of their lives. Some aren't.)

By the way, don't feel too alone about the insecure nature of our work. At least we know it is and can plan for it. People in other lines of business, thinking they're secure and basing their families future on it, are getting let go daily. Many shortly before they could retire.

Even out in the "real world" you can't sit back too much.

SIMPLE

Earlier I mentioned the wisdom of keeping your life simple, especially at the beginning. Please heed this advice. I've seen too many actors over-extend themselves at the first sign of success only to find themselves seriously in debt a year or two later.

Actors are freelance employees. That means we are hired for the job and when it's over, we're unemployed. Our next job might be tomorrow, next week, next month, or who-knows-when. Obviously, we have to plan ahead.

The easiest and best way to do that is to stay out of debt. Expand your lifestyle as your career and bank balance also expand. Get that bigger apartment and new car when you can afford it, not just when you can borrow the money. There is a difference.

One of the biggest problems facing people today is stress. Daily life and dealing with the vicissitudes of this business are tough enough. Don't make it harder on yourself by trying to maintain a lifestyle you're not financially comfortable with yet. If it's important to you, you'll get there. Just don't push it. Earn it.

There's another very pragmatic reason to stay out of severe debt. To audition well, you've got to be free to experiment, free to fail. You can't do that if you desperately *need* every job you go up for. It's the kiss of death and reads like a neon sign.

Besides, it takes all the enjoyment out of it. This business can be great fun or it can drive you crazy. The more you have your "house in order," the easier you'll be with your interviews and auditions, which will lead to more bookings, which will create a fatter bank account.

So handling your debt, lightening up and enjoying life a bit more, is actually great for your business. It might be one of those rare instances where what you would really like to do is also what you *should* do. I'd go for it if I were you.

We also discussed the wisdom of having an alternate source of income, especially at the beginning. Now that we're into the business side of things, let me underline that. At first your business life (making money, paying bills, emergencies, etc.) may be different from your creative, show business life (auditioning, filming, getting agents, pictures, drama coaches, etc.).

That's okay. Blend them when you can. If you are independently wealthy — great. If you're not, get a job that will allow you time to go on interviews and shoot your shows. (That usually means a night job, or one where you don't necessarily have set hours, like real estate or script reading.)

As we all know, some actors make tons of money, others make very little. Until you know where you are going to fall in that spectrum, keep the bottom line covered. Don't rely on hopes.

INVESTING

They say it's never too early to start investing and are they ever right. Like in everything else, if we have to start small, we do, then grow as we can.

One simple little action that so many people over look is how quickly small amounts can add up. It's also a great place to start. If you put just

$20 a week in a savings account, in a year you'll have over a thousand dollars. You're not even going to miss it, but next thing you know, you've got some money in the bank.

If you can do more, do it, but do it regularly. That's the secret. ($50 a week will give you $2,600 plus interest in a year's time. Not bad.)

After you've been acting a few years, you'll find that you receive a lot of checks every week. (Checks for shooting, residuals, holding fees, etc.) Not all of them are big but they add up.

One little trick that worked well for me was to take $10 per check and put it in another account. It didn't matter if the check was for $15.00 or $1,500, I'd take $10 from each and put it away. I didn't miss the money at all and was amazed by how it grew. Give it a try. I think you'll be pleased.

Get an IRA going as soon and as young as you can, if you haven't already. If you have it already, keep it up. Through the wonders of compound interest, $2,000 a year (paid even in small payments, if you wish) can be worth a fortune by the time you are ready to retire.

When you start making more money, move up to a Roth IRA; you can invest more in that one. This is a great way to invest in the future without putting an undo strain on the present.

The very best thing you can do for yourself is to stop paying rent as soon as you can. That means you'll have to buy something; a house, a condo, a trailer... something. Whatever you buy will appreciate, which can later be used as a down payment for something even greater.

The important part is getting started. Of course, that can also be the toughest... you have to come up with the initial down payment. Surprisingly enough, there are many ways to do this.

Some lending institutions have very creative ways to deal with problems like this. Look into them. Ask. See if they can accommodate your current financial situation. If not, you've just learned what one of your new goals is.

Please keep reputable in this. If something seems too good to be true, it probably is. Deal with tried and true companies. You don't want to end up in trouble to a "shark."

Many times, house payments are actually cheaper than rent. Besides the appreciation, the main boon to owning something is that the interest on your mortgage payments is tax-deductible, (For the first 20 years or so, that will represent 90% of your payment.) With rent, you're just throwing it down a hole.

If you have friends or family that are a bit more financially comfortable than you currently are, perhaps they'd go into business with you? They pay the down payment, you pay the monthly payments, live in the place and take care of it. After a predetermined time, you could sell the house and split the profits. (Or if things have gone well for you, you could buy them out. They still make their money, you get a house. Win-win.)

Trust me on this one. I bought my first house when I was 24 and it has been, far and away, the best investment I ever made.

Sometimes good intentions aren't enough. Sometimes you actually should know what you're doing. I would suggest that you educate yourself about money. You don't want to find yourself in a position where what's going on with your finances is above your head.

Even if you just read a couple of Suze Ormon's books, you'll get a healthy, informed way of looking at money. The more you know, the less vulnerable you'll be.

If you start doing very well, you might want to hire a financial adviser, but you should still know enough about it all to understand the options that will be given you. You should also get a monthly accounting of how each of your investments is doing and exactly where your money is, what's it's doing and why, and you *should read it!*

This lesson was learned the hard way by the actress Patty Duke. She had a TV series for years when she was a young girl, where she played twins. Since she played both parts, she worked twice as hard as anyone else with a series.

The considerable money she made was entrusted to a financial planner who was also an old friend of Patty and her mother. How much safer could you get?

That's what Patty thought. She trusted him implicitly and didn't question a thing. The planner, however, was having financial problems of his own. Some of his investments went "south," so he used Patty's money to bail himself out. I'm sure he intended to pay her back after he got solvent again but that never seemed to happen.

She lost everything. Everything! After an Academy Award, a hit TV series and numerous movies, Patty found herself quite successful, in her early thirties… and broke.

Financially, she had to start all over. Fortunately, Patty is a bright, talented lady and she was able to do that, but isn't it too bad that she had to?

Let us take a lesson here. Don't trust your money to anyone totally! Always keep the reins yourself and always know your financial "big picture."

You will learn that not only by reading your monthly financial reports but by asking questions. Anything you don't understand — ask. Please, never think that asking questions is a sign of weakness. It's not. *Not asking* is.

Keep yourself in the loop. It is, after all, your loop.

BESIDES MONEY

Believe it or not, there's more to business than money. (Money's just one of the ways to keep score.)

One area that success in show business shares with other businesses is that of personal relationships. It is a key ingredient in forging good business relations and should be handled with serious but gentle attention.

Make sure you are thought of as you wish to be. Be considerate of everyone. This year's secretary is next year's casting director. The actor that you've been competing with all year may be directing pictures in the not-too-distant future.

Remember, as an actor, you are in the position where you will have to be repeatedly chosen over others. Your life's work depends on this. Anything you can do to make their choice of you easier, is a wonderful thing. Situate yourself for success, not only in your own mind and plans, but in the way you're perceived by others.

No one would think of opening a restaurant without advertising to let people know it was there, yet actors will try to compete with hundreds of other actors and never think of advertising themselves. I'm not talking billboards here, just getting your name out. Producers, directors, and casting people have to know you exist. This can be done a number of ways.

When you sign with an agent, make sure a blurb gets put in *Variety* or the *Hollywood Reporter* announcing it. (They do that.) Postcards with your picture on one side are not all that expensive. Perhaps they could be sent to casting people and ad agencies to also announce that you have just signed with such-and-such agency. Your agents should also be telling everyone that they should meet their new client — you.

This is laying the ground work, getting your name and picture around before you've even done anything. Once you start working, repeat the process. You can also gently encourage your agents to mention your victories.

If you've done something really good, send the postcards with air dates and times, Don't forget to thank the people responsible for you getting the job: your agent, the casting director, and anyone else involved.

Carry this formula with you until you get big enough to hire a publicist to do it for you, but even then, just like with money, make sure you are aware of what's being done in and with your name.

In this business *you* are the commodity. Keep yourself suitable for an instant sale and interesting enough to be marketed at the highest level. Aim as high as you can. You'll never know how high that can be unless you give it a shot. Go for it!

WRAP UP

Even in show business, you are not "on" all the time. (At least I hope you're not!) What matters as much as what you *can* do, is what you *are*. This is the person people meet everywhere except at auditions, where you are the character you're auditioning for.

Some of the most beneficial business contacts are met in the course of everyday life: at parties, restaurants, friends of friends, dinners, screenings, etc. If people find you friendly and interesting, you've taken the first step toward meeting them again, casually or at interviews. You never can tell.

Be the best you can be, on and off camera. You get what you dwell on. Face it all as a business, a good, healthy business… and that's exactly what you'll end up with.

CHAPTER 22

LIFE OFF THE SET

People spend a lot of time and attention planning for their businesses and feel that it's time well spent. Very few, however, devote even half that amount of attention to the planning of their lives. They figure they're going to sleep eight hours, work eight hours, and the remainder will be devoted to family, chores, and television. Weekends are for more chores, sports, and the occasional short trip. What's to plan?

Once again, the unique nature of show business throws those numbers off a bit. Actually, the only one that applies is the eight hours sleep. You will not be working eight hours a day. When you do work it will be ten to 12 hours a day. When you're not, it could be zero, or maybe an hour or two if you have interviews.

That leaves you with a lot of time unaccounted for. Since this time is going to make up the bulk of your life, it should be handled wisely, both for productivity and enjoyment.

Show business may be the focal point of your life but it is not your life, it is your work. Please make your life more well-rounded than that. By concentrating solely on show business, you're cutting off a large portion of life's experience.

The world is vast. The number of interesting things to explore is endless. Expand your horizons and your pursuits. It will make you a more interesting person which will attract more interesting people to you which can be a great source of enjoyment. Also, the more depth you have as a person, the more you can bring to the characters you'll be portraying.

251

ROLE MODELS

Business is not the only place for role models. Life is, as well. While few would actually want to change lives with anyone, there are areas of people's lives that might bear emulating.

You might, for example, like the relationship someone has with his wife and kids, or the way someone always looks so sharp. You may admire how someone never seems to be in a hurry, never harried, yet still manages to accomplish as much, or more, than you do. And how about the person who has had so much adversity but is still able to stay positive and manages to thoroughly enjoy her life?

Borrow what you can from these people and make them your own. Try to capture the spirit behind the actions. These are good, positive steps toward creating the life and lifestyle that will make you fulfilled, happy and proud.

Fully satisfying lives seldom happen by accident. Some thought needs to go into them. Like complaining, happiness is also a habit, and a contagious one at that. It's well worth the time to realize what you want and need in your life, then set about making it happen. Happiness in your life should be as much a goal as success in business.

PLANNING

So, what can you do in those off hours? Well, you could grow; read books, learn why classics are called classics; finish your education or expand on the one you've got; enjoy a sport or two, keep healthy and fit, work out; get involved with a local theater (act, design and build sets, direct, etc.). There's painting, music, writing, and on and on.

You're a creative sort or you wouldn't be going down this road in the first place. Create your own list. What could you do? If money's a little tight (or if you're really planning ahead), you could also find some room on that list for another occupation (not instead of acting, in conjunction).

At the mere mention of a back-up occupation, many will say, "That's just being negative. You've got to have faith."

Well, yes, to an extent. We've already discussed the wisdom of being "free to fail," free to try things. Actually, let's just make that freedom in general. Sometimes it's hard to imagine when you're having to struggle to make it from week to week.

Harrison Ford had the right idea. Before acting took off for him, he worked as a carpenter and enjoyed it. He was getting by just fine.

After he had done his first few acting jobs, offers from low-budget pictures started coming in, offering him, basically, nothing. He figured he'd done enough work for the experience, now he was doing it for a living and the criteria was very clear. If they couldn't pay him more than he was making as a carpenter, they had to find themselves another actor. It just didn't make business sense.

Even in show business, it's important to live with your head, not just your heart.

In good times, prepare for bad times. Pay off credit cards, car payments, lines of credit or other indebtedness when you can. Having a good credit rating established and some wiggle room in your credit card limits can be very helpful when things turn a little slow.

SUPPORT
Earlier we discussed the wisdom of keeping positive friends around you and how harmful the drain of negativity can be. This awareness is even more important in the picking of a spouse or someone you may live with. This person will have more influence on you and your happiness than anyone, so make sure it's positive.

You can help the odds on this a few ways. First, take a good look at your relationship. Is it easy? Do you have to work at it? How hard? Is your partner supportive of what you're doing? Are you supportive of what they're doing? Is home a safe haven?

Support, comfort, and understanding from home is the most important of all.

It's very important that your partner knows about the various ramifications of show business. They need to know the risks, the hours, the lack of security. The rewards are obvious, the down-side isn't.

I remember an embarrassing example of this very well. I was on *General Hospital* and we were in the middle of a rough show. We'd been shooting since 8:00 that morning, and by 8:00 p.m. we still had a third of the show to do. It was going to be a long day and a late night.

A woman had just been hired that day to be one of our new makeup artists. She was thrilled to be a part of the show and didn't mind the hours at all… until her husband started calling. Where was she? Where was his dinner? Why the hell was she still there?

This was a man who didn't understand show business at all. She explained that we were shooting late and that she'd be home as soon as we finished but she didn't know for sure when that would be.

He went crazy. He told her she had to be tough with her new bosses or else they'd push her around and take advantage of her, as they obviously (to him) were that night.

She kept trying to explain, he kept calling every half hour… then it really broke open. He came down to the studio. He stormed onto the set, a large bull of a man, and started telling everyone off. He grabbed his wife, who was practically hysterical by this time, and physically took her away.

It was very sad. A dream had just come true for her and was just as quickly dashed because he didn't know what her job entailed. I doubt if she ever worked in the business again. I would also be surprised if they were still married.

Make sure your partner knows as much as you do about the peculiarities of this business; that you could no more walk out on a shoot before you were finished than you could walk out in the middle of a play you were in. It just isn't done.

Some shoots are easy and fun, some aren't, and the filming takes exactly as long as it takes. No one really knows more than that. We deal with it.

Your partner must realize that late nights, like the above example, do happen now and then. What you really want is to be greeted by a loving, understanding person who knows you've had a very rough day — not be yelled at or have hurt feelings because of the lateness of the hour.

Make sure everyone is on the same page and understands. Once again, the fewer surprises the better... for *both* of you.

TRAVEL

In order to effectively grow as a person, it's important to know what the possibilities are. Travel not only lets you see how other people live and to get other points of view on life, but you'll continually run into great ideas you can incorporate into your own life.

Get out of the country every chance you get. International travel broadens your experience and gives you more of a "citizen of the world" viewpoint. If that's not possible at the moment, get out of town. Explore your state.

Movement and experience are the key words here. It actually doesn't matter what you are doing as long as you do something. Inertia is a killer. It's also boring.

If you're selling furniture in Cleveland, it doesn't matter if you are living exactly like your folks did or that the structure of your life is just like that of your friends. You may meet at the same bar for "happy hour" like you have for years, having the same bowling league night, etc. It can be very safe and very pleasant.

But it's probably not going to play out that way if you are in show business. Knowing how different people live and act is important, and not just reading about it but seeing and experiencing it. This understanding will not only give your characters more depth and richness but you, too.

Actually, if you hang around show business any time at all, travel won't be something you have to work at. It'll be done for you. Over the years location shooting has taken me to nearly every state, Canada, Mexico, England, France, and Italy.

The only thing better than traveling is getting paid to do it.

WRAP UP

Hopefully, your life will be as interesting and successful as your career. To bring this about, keep yourself alert and aware. Be free enough to take advantage of possibilities as they arise, both personal and professional.

The simpler you can make your life, the easier this is accomplished. Edit down your possessions every once in a while. Even that can become a burden.

Surround yourself with positive, loving people and make your world as comfortable as you can. You will never regret the attention you put to that end.

"Life should NOT be a journey to the grave with the intention of arriving safely in an attractive and well preserved body, but rather to skid in sideways, champagne in one hand, strawberries in the other, body thoroughly used up, totally worn out and screaming WOO HOO — what a ride!"

WRAP UP

The following is a list of thoughts I sent my son as he embarked on an acting career. I am pleased to share them with you.

Many of these points have been covered in depth in the book but, because they all are vital, let's just underline a few.

The following is my personal list for being a good actor and an even better person.

Thoughts to Live By

Not necessarily in this order:

Do not act like a "star." People, especially in the business, know who a star is and who isn't. If you have to try to convince them — you aren't.

Loyalty. Be good and true to the people who are being good to you. Never take that for granted, even when it's inconvenient.

Keep your word. Many people forget how appreciated it is to be able to count on someone actually doing what they say they are going to do. Be one of those people. Be consistent and truthful. It'll amaze them.

Keep your personal life as simple as possible. Save the drama for your work. If anyone "needs" you more than you need them — run.

Keep good care of money matters. Keep your monthly nut as low as possible. You must be free to try things, to experiment, to reach. You won't have that freedom if you don't know how you are going to pay your rent or feed your new baby at home.

Never be in a position where you *have* to have this part. That makes for a desperate actor and desperate actors can be spotted a mile away no matter how good they are. They are also never hired.

No one was ever hired out of pity and never will be. Being broke and "in need" will only show the casting people that you are not handling your life very well, so why should they think you could handle their project very well? They won't. They want someone confident, able, secure, and solid. Someone they can cast and never have to worry about again. Feeling sorry for someone does not fit in that category.

Do not borrow money from anyone except the bank and even then, only in dire necessity or when buying a house. (After your career is off and running.) Even if you pay your friend back, it still puts you in a crowd you don't particularly want to be in. There are those who borrow money from their friends and those who don't – period. Don't have people dread running into you (and, yes, it can happen to someone even as charming as you).

And what happens if something doesn't come through or goes awry and you can't pay it back on time? ("Stuff" happens all the time, you know?) Then you've just stiffed your friend, which is the first, if not the last, step in losing that friend. It's also the start of a reputation. Word gets out and flies around this town and this industry. The evil that you do *will* live after you.

Don't ask, or even permit, someone to do for you what you wouldn't do for them. Stay out of any kind of debt, not just financially, but emotionally and humanly as well.

You have to be good to play this game. Remember that all the young actors and actresses in Los Angeles and New York were the best actors in their schools, their towns, maybe even their states. Then they all get together to play hardball with the big guys on the coasts.

That's what you're in the middle of. Very seldom, if ever, are you going to simply "out act" someone, but you may be better prepared, be more the right type, or may bring a more interesting element to the role, etc. Have respect for your fellow actors. They're going through the same thing you are.

Let me share a personal philosophy with you about all this.

Years ago, I found what to me is a common denominator in everyone who wants to be an actor (actually this holds for most of the performing arts). And that is: There was a time in each of their lives when it was *very* important that they be loved. There was a time when they needed to be appreciated, recognized, made to feel special. (Not wanted, but *needed*!)

Usually this need comes from family, but it can also come from friends, peers at school, etc. The draw to the stage (and/or dance, music) is natural. Applause is a narcotic. Few things give such instant and total gratification as an appreciative audience.

Plus, if the world loves you, Mom or Dad (or even a spouse) would have to love you, too, right? If everyone else loves you, how can they not? Visible success is a great pay-back to people who have hurt you or shunned you. (Living well is the best revenge.)

I mean this across the board; Robert Redford, Jim Carrey, Julia Roberts, Tom Hanks, Jodie Foster — name somebody — like me, like you. At one point or another in our lives it was *very* important for us to get the attention performing can bring.

But all of us don't continue to live our lives that way. What happens after one is attracted to this business is up to the individual player. Most of us get ourselves together and grow up. It's no longer necessary that we be loved by everyone. Some, however, never outgrow this "need" (love me, love me) and are the petulant, insecure, neurotic

261

actors you read about in the tabloids. Others of us, who go through this period, realize, after we've made our individual peace with our individual "needs," that we really enjoy this business and, if we're good at it, decide to make it our profession.

Sometimes it may seem like everyone is against you. Not true. Everyone involved in the casting process *really* wants you to succeed. They're casting because they need an actor to play this role. They want you to be so good that you leave no doubt in anyone's mind that you should be the one to play it.

It's an age-old adage, but it's true. "The only truly original thing that you can bring to a role that no one else can bring — is you." Use your own approach, your own personality, your own sense of humor, maybe even a personal petty foible or two to color your characters.

Emulate and learn from others more successful than you, don't try to imitate them. Whatever they're doing has already been done — by them! The gauntlet is going to be passed to whomever can take it from here.

Avoid negative people. There's a lot of negativity in this business. People complaining, putting others down, bitching about the unfairness of most anything, gleefully spreading hurtful rumors, etc. Do not let them be a part of your life. If they already are, phase them out. Let them go.

Life in this business and maintaining a positive attitude is hard enough. Being surrounded by negativity makes it much harder. If you feel yourself becoming one of these people — get out of the business. I mean that sincerely. This business is not for everyone. The uncertainty of it and the rejection drives some people crazy.

If you are one of these people, don't view it as a failure — be glad you were astute enough to recognize it before you spent a major part of your life being unhappy. Go back to school. Chalk this up as an interesting chapter in your life, one you'll always have, then move on.

Let show business be your occupation, not your life. Always have something else going. It will make you a much more secure and interesting person. Learn, grow, experience things. You're in the business of interpreting life. The more life experiences you have, the better you'll be at it. Knowledge and experience are never wasted, none of it. It makes you a deeper, more well-rounded individual and that makes for a much more interesting actor than one who knows nothing but theater and movies.

Don't procrastinate. Do as much of what has to be done today, because tomorrow you may get your series and not have time to do them.

(This incidentally, is an example of the narcotic of show biz and keeps people in it even with few or no rewards; the next call could change your life. And it could!)

Watch TV, movies, and commercials with awareness. Know who's doing what and why. Why is someone considered good? What are they doing? Try to see as many plays, programs or commercials as you can that you didn't get. What did the actor who did get it do that you didn't? What can you learn from that?

You don't want to imitate or act like another person, but there may be attributes, attitudes, maybe even movements that you may integrate into your own abilities.

Know what made and is making the great, great. Is there anything there that could be added to your personal arsenal?

Keep in touch with family and friends. Make sure those you love know you love them. Don't set yourself up for regrets. Besides, a good support group comes in very handy.

Please don't make money, fancy clothes, and fast cars your goal. A young actor with his act together is much more impressive than one who is trying to impress. People who throw their money around and go in debt to drive a fancy car are certainly not respected for those traits — rather, they are generally taken advantage of. Do not confuse people who let you buy all the drinks you can for them as friends. They are not.

No one expects actors at the beginning of their careers to have all the trappings of success. There is dignity in the struggle. Nothing that comes too easily is essentially worthwhile. Let the spoils of success come and grow with your success. This is the main instance where it is very important to *be* the part, not act the part.

Remember, most regrets come from "not having done something," very few from actions actually taken. Inaction and inactivity are villains.

And finally, you'll hear this to death but it's true, "Have fun with it."

Show business is one of the toughest businesses in the world. There is a huge "luck factor" and you never know which side of that you are going to be on. But if you handle it wisely, there is an amazing sense of freedom in it all.

Keep your attitude positive, be true to your mentors, learn as much as you can about everything, hang out with people who are smarter than you. Learn what a professional in this business means, then become one. Don't do anything you wouldn't want shown on TV — it just may be.

Remember, this year's secretary is next year's casting director. Be courteous to everyone. Grow in the business together. Don't burn your bridges. Don't be a "flake." Be the one people can count on.

Don't dwell on all this. Read it over a few times, think about it, then let it go and live your life as naturally and as interestingly as you can.

You'll find these points will be there when you need them.

All the very best to you. You're heading down an historic road. Be proud of it. Be worthy of it and... have fun with it. And please remember how lucky we are. There are few who, at the end of the day, will have enjoyed themselves as much as we have.

Steve Carlson has been a working actor for nearly 40 years. In his varied career he has been a "regular" on three TV series (*General Hospital* on ABC, *The Young & the Restless* on CBS, and *A New Day in Eden* on Showtime). He has re-occurred in many more, has guest-starred in over 50 TV episodes and stared or co-starred in ten feature films.

Over the years he has also become one of the most successful commercial actors in the country having filmed or supplied the voice for over 400 TV & radio commercials.

Steve is currently semi-retired in the wilds of Southern Oregon.

Mr. Carlson also does seminars based on the information in this book. For more information, he can be reached at:

Steve Carlson
c/o Michael Wiese Productions
11288 Ventura Blvd. #621
Studio City, CA 91604

or by Email: *carlson@connpoint.net*

Books by Steve Carlson

Hitting Your Mark: Special 2nd Edition
Making a Life – and a Living – as a Film Actor

The Commercial Actors Guide
Creating, Building, and Maintaining a Career (Heinemann, 2005)

MICHAEL WIESE PRODUCTIONS

Since 1981, Michael Wiese Productions has been dedicated to providing both novice and seasoned filmmakers with vital information on all aspects of filmmaking. We have published more than 70 books, used in over 500 film schools and countless universities, and by hundreds of thousands of filmmakers worldwide.

Our authors are successful industry professionals who spend innumerable hours writing about the hard stuff: budgeting, financing, directing, marketing, and distribution. They believe that if they share their knowledge and experience with others, more high quality films will be produced.

And that has been our mission, now complemented through our new web-based resources. We invite all readers to visit www.mwp.com to receive free tipsheets and sample chapters, participate in forum discussions, obtain product discounts — and even get the opportunity to receive free books, project consulting, and other services offered by our company.

Our goal is, quite simply, to help you reach your goals. That's why we give our readers the most complete portal for filmmaking knowledge available — in the most convenient manner.

We truly hope that our books and web-based resources will empower you to create enduring films that will last for generations to come.

Let us hear from you at anytime.

Sincerely,
Michael Wiese
Publisher, Filmmaker

www.mwp.com